BASIC FISHING

BASIC FISHING

Ray Ovington

Stackpole Books

799.11

BASIC FISHING

Library of Congress Cataloging in Publication Data

Ovington, Ray.
  Basic fishing.

  Includes index.
    1. Fishing. I. Title.
SH441.0937   799.1'1   82-5436
ISBN 0-8117-2141-8 (pbk.)   AACR2

Contents

3925

Acknowledgments

THIS IS MY thirty-second book on outdoor recreation. Fourteen of these have been about fishing, the latest being THE TROUT AND THE FLY (New York: Hawthorn, 1978). TACTICS ON TROUT was published by Alfred A. Knopf in 1969. Two books of similar interest were published by the Stackpole Company, INTRODUCTION TO BAIT FISHING (1973) and BASIC FLY FISHING AND FLY TYING (1974). HOW TO TAKE TROUT, published originally by Little, Brown in 1952, has been reprinted and updated by Freshet Press, New York. Since basic fishing information on fishing rigs and techniques is universal, I am indebted to these publishers for the use of information that has been incorporated in this book. Thanks for material concepts and specific information written for this book go also to magazine publishers who have published articles under my name, such as FIELD & STREAM, OUTDOOR LIFE, SPORTS AFIELD, TRUE, ARGOSY, ELKS, THE FLY FISHERMAN, TROUT MAGAZINE, PENNSYLVANIA ANGLER, and many other publications.

I will always be indebted to the NEW YORK WORLD TELE-GRAM AND SUN for publishing my daily column "Outdoors." This assignment offered trips all over the globe and experiences that few could ever hope to be granted.

Thanks, too, to the guides, outfitters, conservation officials, travel agents, tackle retailers, and fellow anglers who have contributed to my experience as a sportsman and angler.

My Dad gets an extra thanks.

Preface

WHY GO FISHING? Fish markets and frozen-food counters have all kinds of fish, cleaned, frozen, and neatly wrapped, as well as packages of precooked fish.

Evidently fishermen want to have fun and test their wits. Deeper than this is the urge to return to nature, to the pond or stream—away from cities and crowds—back to the basic contact with the natural environment.

Most fishing in early times was to obtain food for the family. Today the sport and art of fishing enjoys more than two-hundred years of refinement, both in aesthetic appreciation and in the improvement of tackle and technique. You can go forth with a pole cut from a sapling tree, a string, a penny hook, and a can of worms, and you'll catch fish. But the real joy is in using beautifully designed rods, reels, lines, terminal tackle, and a myriad of artificial flies and lures. With these you will not only catch more fish but also have more fun. There is nothing like going astream or on a pond with the right gear, knowing how it works, and armed with the tricks, tips, and hints to make your fishing trip more productive.

Where do you fish? Almost anyplace where there is water! Some of the sportiest fish may not reside in the lake or stream nearest your house. But unless you live in the desert, a short ride will take you to some form of natural water. And there will be fish there. If you live in the Northeast, for example, a little nearby pond may contain catfish, panfish, or even bass. There will be trout in the cool streams and deep lakes—perhaps even landlocked salmon. Atlantic salmon fill the rivers of Maine and the eastern Canadian provinces along with smallmouth bass, pike, and muskies. If you live in the Southern states you'll find good largemouth bass, catfish, and panfish in almost every river. In the Midwest you go for bass and trout, pike and muskies. On the West Coast you'll encounter sea-run cutthroat, steelhead, rainbow trout, and many species of salmon. There are good bass lakes in the states of Oregon and Washington.

Fishing gives you the opportunity to engage in an activity where there are few constants. The only restrictions in fishing are the game laws. Weather and seasonal conditions are never the same, nor are the types and kinds of water, nor fish habits, moods, feeding and striking abilities. . . .

You'll find that each kind of fishing offers its own particular thrills. When you are able to cast a dainty dry fly over the glassy trout pool of a mountain stream and entice a trout into leaping for it, there is a sensation that will be long remembered. The bass that bursts out of a crop of lily pads to pounce on your plug will make you jump in response. The little sunfish that grabs a worm dangled over the end of the dock can be a lot of fun as well. Many of the world's most sophisticated anglers still find a special thrill in panfishing even though they have been used to fighting giant tuna or big-deep monsters. The first time you view an Atlantic salmon jumping over a twelve-foot waterfall you'll wonder what that fish can do to your frail fly-fishing tackle.

There are many fishing adventures ahead of you, whether a simple jaunt to a neighborhood lake or a well-planned trek to distant waters. Fishing, you'll find, is full of wonderful surprises.

YOU HAVE IN your hands a book that tells you what you need to know to go freshwater fishing with the right equipment, how to use that equipment properly, and how to enjoy catching fish.

The instructions and diagrams are presented as simply as possible. The best way to proceed is to read the book through once to get a general idea. Then, with your tackle in front of you, you can begin to experiment with assembly, casting, etc., to start to develop know-how and coordination. Finally, read the relevant sections of the book through again, put the book down, and proceed from memory.

If you have a friend or uncle or dad (or sister or mom) at hand, have your helper read aloud from the book while you perform each step. From then on it's a matter of perfecting and smoothing your action, as you would do if you were learning golf or tennis or archery.

At first you may be all thumbs, but that stage will pass quickly.

Learn by watching and talking to other fishermen. Visit your local tackle store or rod and gun club. Get to know the experts. Ask them for help. They'll help you

Good luck!

1

Tackle Selection

THE PURCHASE OF tackle, like the buying of anything important, should be made only after careful planning and shopping. Over a period of time you'll discover brands and types of equipment that you prefer. You'll also wear out or lose equipment and have to replace it.

Good fishing tackle is not cheap. You'll find that buying good quality is, in the long run, the most inexpensive way to go. There is nothing so discouraging as malfunctioning equipment.

After a few years or even one full season of fishing, you'll develop tastes for specific kinds of gear. Care for it well, and it will survive many years of hard use. You'll be free to concentrate on your fish finding and presentation techniques instead of fussing with your equipment.

This book outlines some basic specifications, general as they are (and must be), to guide you in choosing gear for various specific fishing demands. Go to the tackle store and look over the gear on the shelves and counters. Talk over your fishing prospects with the tackle clerk and get his opinion. Buy your tackle in a fishing-tackle store where there are specialists to help you. There is a big difference between the service at such stores and that offered by the discount outlets.

Also, the specialized tackle store is a mecca for other anglers and members of the local rod and gun club. Many fishermen will be happy to help you, including sharing where-to-go information for the best fishing.

The real fun of tackle buying is in lure selection. Find the inventive genius in an endless number of lures. At first you'll be tempted to buy many more lures than you actually need. Here again, refinement and discrimination will develop as you learn by fishing.

2

Spin Fishing

OPEN THE BOX with your new reel in it and before you do anything else, fill out the guarantee and carefully read the directions.

Read them again.

Suppose you have bought a standard open-face type reel (see Figure 1). The spools for this type of reel are instantly detachable and make it possible to have two or more reels in one, since at any given time you can switch from one spool to another for varied lure weights. In the better stores the clerk usually spools on the line for you, but if you have to do it yourself make sure you roll the line on without a twist in any of the revolutions (see Figure 2).

For trout and bass load one spool with four- or six-pound test line and another with an eight- or ten-pound test line. These are sufficient to handle all weight lures.

The manual tells you to thread the line through the closed bail on the reel and through the groove made to carry the line. Next attach the reel in line with the guide on the first handle section of

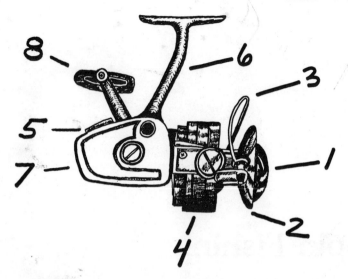

Figure 1. TYPICAL OPEN-FACE REEL FOR SPINNING

1. **Drag adjust nut (spools are instantly removable for quick line change).**
2. **Spool.**
3. **Bail pickup.**
4. **Roller.**
5. **Antireverse lever.**
6. **Frame foot mounting.**
7. **Gear housing.**
8. **Crank.**

the rod. Then take the tip section of the rod, rub the ferrule on your nose to oil it a bit, and insert the section into the butt-section ferrule by first lining up the line guides so you will not need to twist the sections once they're together. Twisting the sections forms grooves that will cause much trouble later and also weakens the bond of ferrule to end section. When taking the rod apart, be careful not to twist it for the same reason. Do not bend the rod when pulling sections apart. This strains the joints and tends to bend or loosen the ferrules.

Now, with the rod assembled, the reel mounted in the center of the handle, and the line fed from the reel, pull out line with the drag (see *glossary*) on, and thread the line through the rod guides (or *line guides*). Once the line is through the tip-top guide, attach a snap swivel to the line using a clinch knot. (See the discussion of knots in TERMINAL TACKLE.)

Now you are ready to cast.

For practice, tie on a lightweight object to simulate a weighted lure. A stick will do, or anything handy that is not more than an ounce in weight. Draw out about a foot of line, stand up, and hold the rod out in front of you. Pick up the line in the index finger of the hand holding the rod and open the bail. Point the rod up slightly. The weight is now dangling from the rod tip.

Let go of the line. The weight will drop. Look at the reel. There is no backlash. Only the needed amount of line came from the spool (this is the basic principle of the spinning reel).

Casting the spinning rod is as easy as what you have just performed. Repeat the process up to the time of line release—pause—and then release it again to get the feel.

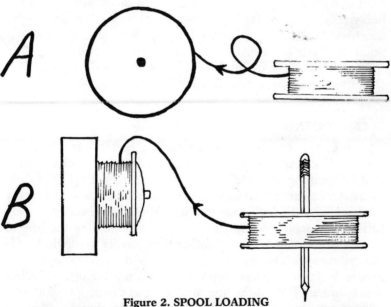

Figure 2. SPOOL LOADING
A. Wrong. If you load the spool this way, you will cause loops that tangle when you cast.
B. Right. Spool the line on directly. Wind the line on by reeling in with the reel mounted on the butt section of the rod for ease of operation. Have your partner hold the line spool and let it revolve on a pencil. With the line wound on this way, with even tension, you are ready to fish!

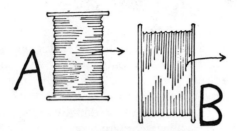

Figure 3. SPOOL TYPES
A. The conventional barrel position for unwinding the line.
B. The open-end position of the same barrel that allows line to coil off the end of the rim.

To cast, do a practice dry run. With the line in your finger and the bail open, lift the rod from the horizontal to the vertical with a bit of a swing upward and then bring it down again. Feel the line pull at your finger? Do this several times. On one of the downward swings let go of the line at just about the horizontal point. See how the weight went out in front of you?

To reel back in you merely crank the reel handle and the bail closes over the line and in it comes!

SPIN CASTING

Spinning is the most modern casting tackle. Developed in Europe fifty years ago it was brought to America prior to World War II. Spinning reels were developed on a very simple principle in order to create an easier way of casting than was available for lure fishing with the conventional bait-casting reel. By merely turning the reel spool sideways, and thus allowing the line to loop off the end of the spool rather than having to unwind it off the rolling spool, a completely new system was developed (see Figure 3). In one simple step the age-old trouble of backlashes was eliminated. With the line falling off as casting pressure dictated, a frictionless flow of line was possible, thereby allowing lighter lures to be cast accurately and far. For many years it looked as if spinning was going to put bait casting on the museum shelves. But bait casting has not only survived, it has become more popular. Each of the two methods has its own place in angling.

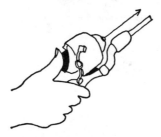

Figure 4. HAND POSITION FOR CLOSED-FACE REEL
This is the way to grip the closed-face reel mounted on a bait-casting rod with an offset handle. Your thumb falls easily on the lever that releases the line on the forward swing of the cast.

The open-face reel was the original type of spinning reel. This was followed by the closed-face reel, which also has become quite popular. The author still likes the open-face for many reasons which will become obvious through the instruction. (For instance, the placing of the face over the front of the spool restricts the line flow.)

The spinning rod is different from the bait-casting or fly rod. Since the reel hangs down (the open-face reel) under the cork handle, the line guides are mounted on the bottom of the rod. The line guides are very large near the reel, gradually becoming

Figure 5. PUSH-BUTTON REEL
The push-button reel is a spinning reel with a cone-covered stationary spool similar to the open-face model. Instead of a bail pickup, this requires picking up the line with the index finger. The push-button reel has a lever with which to connect the reel-in sequence and activate it. It comes equipped with star drag and antireverse handle and is easy to use with the conventional light bait-casting rod and the proper weights of spinning rods. This is a good rig for bait fishing as well as trolling and lure casting.

smaller as they approach the tip of the rod (see Figure 7). The line feeding out from the edge of the spool is coming off in coils. Too rapid a restriction of the line would cut down on the speed. Also of importance in casting is the flexing action of the rod. Figure 8 shows this action.

Figure 6. ADJUSTING DRAG ON CLOSED-FACE REELS
To reduce drag tension, back up handle ¼ turn. To regain original drag tension, turn handle forward.

SYNCHRO-DRAG
The star drag is synchronized with another instantly adjustable line drag control built into the handle. No need to touch the drag wheel when a big fish makes a desperate lunge—just turn the handle back to reduce line drag instantly.

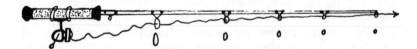

Figure 7. LINE GUIDES ON SPINNING ROD

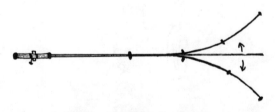

Figure 8. ROD FLEXING
The rod is held at the horizontal position and pressure (up and down by wrist action) is exerted. Flex the tip of the rod and make the weight begin to travel as shown when you make the cast. Flex several times to get the feel of the action. Starting slowly and easily, increase the pressure and note the change necessary in your timing due to the additional pull from the weight of the rod tip. This same pressure is felt when the rod is held at the vertical position.

ROD GRIP

Figure 9 shows the typical spinning rod handle with the reel hanging down. The rod must be gripped with the stem of the reel straddled between the second and third fingers. Grasp the rod gently. Do not develop the habit of a tense hand grip on any tackle, since this will soon tire you. Your index finger controls the cast length merely by pressing on the edge of the spool, thus stopping the line. Try it. This is similar to the action of the thumb in line control in bait casting, but much easier. Grasp the rod with your thumb resting comfortably on top. Do not twist your wrist so that you can see your fingernails.

With the proper rod grip, you are now ready to cast. You can practice the following casting and retrieving routines in any yard or park–but make sure you use a lure without hooks!

CASTING SEQUENCE (refers to Figure 10)

All through the sequence the forearm is kept virtually horizontal and all the action is in the hand and wrist.

1. The initial power lift from the horizontal position of the rod.

Figure 9. GRIPPING THE SPINNING ROD
The right hand is gripping the spinning rod with the stem of the reel between the second and third fingers. The grip should be relaxed so that the wrist is free to move. The forefinger grasps the line lightly. At the moment of release of the line, the forefinger lets go of the line and the line slips or is pulled off the finger section from the pressure of the cast.

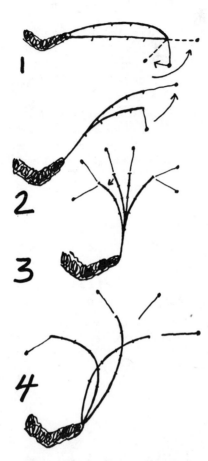

Figure 10. CASTING SEQUENCE

The hand and the rod are both "flat." As the arrow indicates, the rod begins to bend as the upward pressure of the hand is initiated. After a brief swing inward, the lure begins to move outward.

2. The halfway position showing the rod flexing and the lure moving upward. During this stage your hand is not moving but the rod is reacting to the pressure that is exerted on it.

3. Back pressure is applied as your hand reaches the vertical position in a pressure push. The arrow shows the direction of the rod-flex and the path of the lure's weight as it swings down.

4. With the lure down and the rod bent to the extreme back position, snap the rod gently forward, causing a reverse of the movement of the preceding diagram. The lure travels up and over the tip of the rod and when it reaches its final point, as shown, you release the line by allowing it to slip off your index finger. (In the case of the closed-face reel you merely push the button to release the line at this point.)

The rod falls and the line releases straight out from the rod tip and line and lure begin to drop down to the water.

The final position of the cast is exactly the same as the beginning—horizontal with the hand and rod "flat" (see Figure 11).

TIMING THE RELEASE

The most difficult part of the spin cast is to learn the timing of the line release. If you let go of the line too soon, the lure will take off into the air all right—but wind will disrupt your direction and distance will be practically impossible to control. Also, there will be much too much slack line on the water which you will have to reel in quickly before a fish strikes, or if you are using a sinking lure in shallow water it will snag on the bottom before you start retrieving. When fishing in shallow water the cast must be flat, and you begin the retrieve a split second before the lure hits the water.

The angle of the lure in relation to the rod is important to note and feel. If you wait too long for the line release, the lure will splash down in front of you, well short of its target.

The straight line in Figure 11 shows the proper direction of the lure from the rod tip. This is the nice flat cast that is directional, saving on slack line, and accurate . . . plus easy to control as to distance.

To control distance, snub the line before the lure begins to fall at the point shown in the diagram. To snub, merely place your index finger on the very lip of the spool. This retards and/or stops the line from coming off the spool (wavy line in Figure 11). If you really snub the line tight, the lure pulls at you and bounces down into the water. Try this a few times to get the feel and you will always be able to control a lure that is headed for the brush

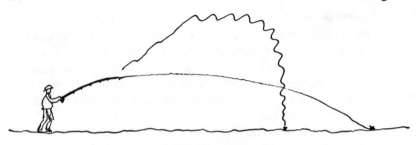

Figure 11. TIMING THE LINE RELEASE

and snags. Believe it or not, you'll soon be controlling those casts to within inches of your selected target.

Don't try to make long-distance casts yet. Get to know your outfit so its operation is second nature to you. One night you may be fishing in total darkness. You'll have to perform all this without being able to see.

The sidewinder cast is essentially the same as the upright. The rod is pointed at the target but instead of bringing it straight up to your eye in the vertical position, you swing it in the horizontal plane, being careful that no one is near you and that you are clear of brush or snags. This cast is used when you want to throw the lure under an overhang or there is a tree limb over your head. Use the vertical cast for most of your fishing though. It's much more accurate.

RETRIEVING THE LINE

The next thing to learn is the retrieving of the line after the cast. Close the bail over the line by cranking the handle. (You will see this happens automatically.) Start to retrieve with the rod in a position just a few inches above the horizontal and the bend of the rod will cushion a sudden pull from a fish. If you like, you can raise your rod almost to the vertical. Personally I think you have better control if you retrieve with the rod at about a two o'clock angle. As the lure comes in close you can gradually lower the rod tip so that the lure remains on the water until the very last moment of pickup.

The horizontal position is good when you are manipulating the rod to give action to the lure. (Do this by pulling back and up suddenly in short jerks and then lowering the rod, making the lure move up and down in the water.)

The retrieve position is diagrammed in Figure 12 (see caption) . . . and retrieving styles are covered later in the section on lake fishing.

STRIKING, PLAYING, AND LANDING

Let's learn about the built-in features of the spinning reel that make playing the fish more fun, easier, and very efficient.

First, preset the drag pressure of the reel spool to just under the breaking strength of the line.

To measure the amount of reserve power in the rod you are using, attach your line to a solid object and back away about fifty feet. Raise the rod tip against the strain of the tied line and bend the rod full against it until the drag lets go and the line goes out from the reel. See? You have a large amount of reserve power, even with a very light rod and line. Now you can feel the amount of power available to use against your fish. The light spinning rod, with its exceptional amount of spring, and the light line are sufficient for playing much bigger fish than you might have thought. Performing this simple experiment will show you a lot about your tackle and its possibilities.

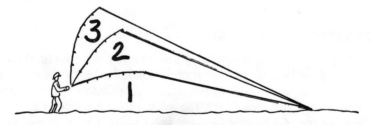

Figure 12. THE RETRIEVE
Rod position 2 is that of the normal retrieve. However, position 3 is also recommended, since the bent rod creates tension against the line for even spooling as well as serving as a cushion against the strike of the fish. Position 1 can be used with sinking lures in shallow water or when it is desired that the lure be kept right on the surface. Positions 2 and 3 keep the line from snagging brush, grass, or rocks.

Now try this. Point the rod straight at the line as it is attached fifty feet out to a solid object. Now pull directly without using the cushion of the rod. The line breaks easily. You must keep that rod tip up, or, if in the horizontal position, back at right angles to the battle.

If you were to have the rod in the down position, and pointing directly at the line (at the fish), when the fish struck the line would break if the fish pulled with more pressure than the pound test of the leader. So you want to use the rod as a cushion.

When the fish takes the bait, or lure, or fly, you strike—i.e. pull back hard on the rod, either up or to the side, to set the hook in the fish's mouth. At just what moment you should strike and how hard varies, and some different striking techniques for different fish will be covered later on. But once you strike and the hook is set and you start playing your fish, you want to transfer as much tension as possible from your line to your rod. And this you do by holding the rod *up*, so that when there's a sudden increase in tension the rod bends, taking it, and relieving the line.

Playing a fish with a bait or spinning rig you use the reel, lowering the rod a bit and reeling in as you do so, then pulling back on the rod, then lowering again and reeling in as you do so, then hauling back again, etc.

Landing your fish you want to avoid swiping at it with your net. Lower that net gently into the water and let the fish slide into it. No sudden moves . . . no desperate lunges.

PUTTING YOUR TACKLE AWAY

Detach the lure from the snap swivel and put it (the lure) back in the tackle box. If you are merely stacking the rig for another trip in a few hours and do not need to break down the rod and put it away, you can attach the swivel to the keeper ring (just ahead of the rod handle on most good rods). This is better than attaching the swivel and snap to the tip-top guide at the end of the rod. Metal-to-metal scratches should be avoided, and that top guide above all others should be guarded against scratching. Do not lean the rod against the wall of the cabin or put it in a place where it will fall over from the wind and be walked on or driven over by a car. Hang it from a string tied to a nail or lay it down in a dry place away from traffic.

To fully break down, detach the snap swivel, put it in its container in the tackle box, rewind the line back onto the reel, and place the line end in the slot in the reel so that the line will not unwind and tangle. If this slot is not built into your reel, use a rubberband kept on the reel shank for this purpose. Wrap the band over the line end as it is wound on the spool.

To break the rod down, gently pull the sections apart. Do not twist. Clean each section, remove the reel, and place the rod in the case and the reel in the box. All is ready for your next fishing trip.

RECOMMENDED SPINNING TACKLE FOR AVERAGE FRESHWATER FISHING

Rod action—the variation from stiff tip to soft-action tip— makes a great deal of difference in the handling of all lure weights. A stiff-tipped rod is needed to cast heavy plugs and spoons into the wind and also to strike hard on big fish and enable the angler to drag the fish through the weeds. For most open-water fishing, and especially in quiet rivers, the light gear will be most suitable. For fast trout stream work, where the fish congregate in the rips, a slightly heavier tip and stronger line is advised even when fishing with light lures.

The specifications in Table 1 are *general* guidelines. They'll

Table 1.

ROD	REEL	FISH SIZE	LINE TEST	LURE WEIGHT
ultralight 5 to 6 ft.	ultralight to light action	small trout, panfish, small bass—short casts	4, 5, 6 lbs.	⅛ to ⅜ oz.
6 to 6½ ft.	light to medium action	medium casts for larger bass and trout, pickerel, etc.	6, 7, 8 lbs.	¼ to ½ oz.
6½ to 7½ ft.	medium to heavy action	big bass, big lake trout, pike—	9, 10 lbs.	½ to 1 oz. or heavier

help you get started, but as you gain experience, paying close attention to the way your rod-reel-line-lure combinations perform in given fishing situations, you'll work up your own set of preferences for rod length, reel action, line test, and lure weight. As you get more expert, for instance, you might want to start going much lighter on your line test to make the playing and landing of your fish more difficult and therefore more sporting.

In any event, don't take tables as gospel. They're to help you get started, get a general idea of what weight lure to rig up with what test line and what kind of rod action – but too many would-be fishermen read the tables and follow them to the letter and think all their problems are automatically going to be solved. They think they never again will have to pay attention to their rig's performance *while they're fishing*. But no two fishermen are alike and no two stream or lake situations are alike. So use the charts and table in this book as guides to get started, but only to get started. The table will never be written that will tell you the exact rod-reel-line-lure combinations for you.

3

Bait Casting

THE ACTION OF the bait casting reel is based on the spool revolving and feeding the line off or taking it back on as the spool is turned by a handle. The modern "multiplying-reel" spool turns about four revolutions to one turn of the handle. A level-wind mechanism in the form of a slot to feed the line on a crossbar was added so that the line would be reeled onto the spool evenly.

The first bait-casting rods (made of split bamboo, then steel, and finally glass, both solid and tubular) had straight cork handles upon which the reel was mounted. In order to make the line control easier, the offset handle was designed, placing the reel in an easier position (see Figure 13).

The line is fed through guides mounted on the top side of the rod.

In the early days lines were made of braided silk, but today braided nylon has become the accepted line to use. For special instances, monofilament line is also used.

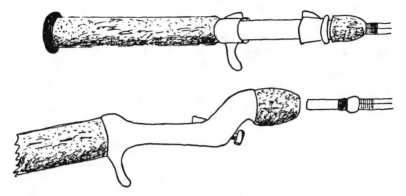

Figure 13. STRAIGHT AND OFFSET HANDLES
On top is the straight-handled rod inherited from many years of tackle development and still preferred by many anglers. On the bottom is the offset handle which allows a lower position for the reel and a better and easier thumb position on the line.

ROD GRIP

The typical offset-handled rod, with the bait-casting reel mounted on the top, leaves the handle free to grasp easily with your thumb resting on the spool (see Figure 14). Do not turn your hand so that you can see your fingernails. The trigger on the

Figure 14. HAND POSITION: BAIT-CASTING REEL
The way to hold the bait-casting rod. The thumb falls conveniently on the line spool for instant and constant control. The grip should be easy, re-laxed, and soft. There is no need for grip tension. Save that energy for the cast and line control.

bottom of the rod handle just under the reel is there for your forefinger to use as a pressurepoint in casting. The thumb rests naturally on the reel spool and touches the line as it should for control during the cast.

There is a drag-control button on some reels in the center of the outside of the spool (see Figure 15). For initial practice sessions it is suggested you tighten the drag just a bit so the spool won't revolve too freely. Later, after you become accustomed to the reel and its actions and develop your own casting style, you can gradually relax the drag and thereby gain more distance in the cast.

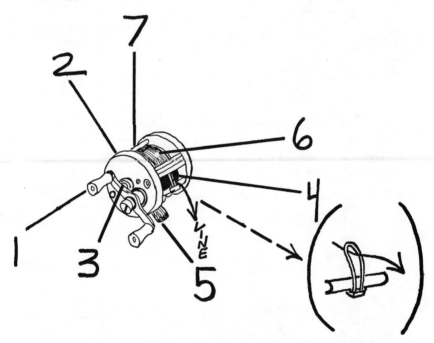

Figure 15: BAIT-CASTING REEL
Typical bait-casting reel complete with level-wind mechanism (slot on crossbar through which line is fed so line reels onto spool evenly). The parts as labelled include:

1. Handle or crank.
2. Head.
3. Drag.
4. Level wind.

5. Cross plate, or foot.
6. Spool.
7. Pillar.

One of the reasons why that drag is there is for trolling. When the rod is left loose in the boat and the drag is set under the pound test of the line and a fish hits, the line will not release.

Bait-casting rod line guides are much smaller than spinning rod line guides simply because the line is fed directly to the guide rather than in a loop. The bait-casting reel is mounted on the top of the rod. The line is fed through the level-wind posts and threaded directly into the first line guide and through to the tip.

Bait-casting rods are made either in one piece or two. The former is more awkward to pack but its action is superior to the two-piece since the ferrule joint interferes with the action. Some rods have a hook-keeper ring mounted just ahead of the handle. If not, hook your lure in the reel bar, not in the line guides, since this will scratch them and thus ruin your line.

CASTING THE TACKLE

The basic difference between spin casting and bait casting involves the operation of the reel and line control. Otherwise, the casting actions are exactly the same as illustrated in the chapter on spin casting.

Remember, with the spinning rod the casting was done with the right hand and the cranking of the reel with the left hand. This required no shift of the rod from hand to hand. The bait-casting reel is mounted so that the handle is on the right, which means that after the cast is made, the rod and reel are quickly shifted to the left hand, and the reeling is done with the right hand.

The most difficult part of bait casting is avoiding backlash. This is done by controlling the line under the pressure of the cast.

With rod, reel, and line set up to cast (as in spin casting: line and lure hanging down from rod tip about six inches), the thumb of the casting (right) hand is held gently on the line spool to keep it from being forced to revolve by the weight of the lure.

Lift your thumb away from the spool and the weight of the lure will pull off line and cause the reel spool to revolve. If you do not stop it from revolving, when the lure hits the floor the reel spool will keep on revolving even though no more line is being

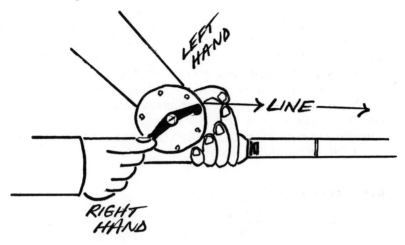

Figure 16. RETRIEVING THE BAIT CAST

pulled off. This is what is known as backlash . . . and just a small example of what can happen during a power cast, forcing you to untangle many yards of snarled, fouled line.

To avoid all this start out easily, feeling your way and getting used to the release of the line and the lure falling to the floor. Stop the spool a split second before the lure hits the floor and you will not have an overlap of line on the spool. Try this several times before you attempt to cast.

Now, holding your thumb on the line spool with more pressure (since the lure will exert pull on the line), vibrate the rod tip up and down. On one of the downward thrusts release the line for an instant and then snub it again with your thumb. The lure will move out from the rod tip somewhat, as in an actual cast.

If your timing was right, there was no backlash.

Do this several times, allowing a longer "cast" each time.

Then try some full-fledged casts, following the same drill as for spin casting except remember to snub the spool (firmly but smoothly) just before the lure lands.

(And don't try right away for distance!)

THE RETRIEVE

After switching the rod from the right hand to the left, slide the left hand forward of the reel. Grasp the incoming line in your thumb and forefinger and maintain a slight tension as you retrieve the line. (See Figure 16.) This keeps the line clean and feeds it onto the reel under even pressure so that it will cast evenly the next time around.

Practice this hand switching and the left-hand-forward position a few times until it becomes easy.

STRIKING, PLAYING, LANDING

Striking, playing, and landing a fish with bait-casting tackle is very similar to doing it with spinning gear, except that your thumb is the final authority over the line on the strike.

When you're playing the fish the reel drag—preset to a test just under the breaking strain of the line—comes prominently into play and helps you in maintaining line control with your right hand on the reel handle (and the rod in your left hand).

4

Fly-Fishing

THE FLY ROD is the longest and bendiest of the three types of rod (see Figure 17), and also the most subtle – requiring a relaxed though accurate feel of the balanced tackle in motion – and a delight to cast with once you've learned.

The lure, a very light fly in comparison with the lures used in bait and spin fishing, merely goes along for the ride. Its weight does not pull the line from the reel. The line and leader can be cast without a fly on the end.

The reel is mounted behind the hand, hanging down. The rod guides are small in diameter, since the line is fed to the first guide from your hand, not directly from the reel.

The reel itself is merely a spool to hold the line (see Figure 18). The fish is not played from the reel unless it is a very big trout, bass, or salmon. The reel is single action.

Lines are made in various sizes and tapers as schematically illustrated in Figure 19. These tapers have a very definite purpose and function (see Figure 19 caption).

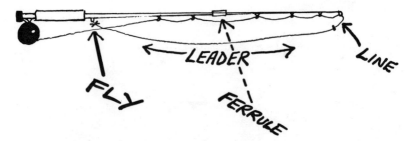

Figure 17. The conventional fly-fishing tackle of rod, reel, line, and leader all set to use with the fly hooked into the fly-keeper ring. The leader is tied onto the line as indicated in the chapter on terminal tackle. Note that the reel is in the "down" position and is not used in the upright position.

Illustrated is the preferred two-piece rod, though it is a bit long for easy carrying and travel. Fly rods also come in three sections. Setting the rod up and being careful with the jointing and unjointing is as important as it is in bait- and spin-casting tackle to keep the rod unscratched, unbent, and always in perfect condition. The handle is of cork. The reel seat is either two rings that slide on the base of the reel or a screw type. The screw type is preferred since the reel cannot accidentally become loose. Rod material is either tubular glass, split bamboo, or graphite. Glass is recommended for the beginner. Good bamboo and graphite rods are quite expensive and really unnecessary until you reach the advanced point of having special needs in rod action.

Leaders, attached to the end of the line, are tapered too, in most cases, to balance the end of the cast and allow the fly to set down properly on the water. They are tapered as thinly as possible to allow freedom of movement to the fly and offer less visibility to the fish. Thus, the fly appears to be natural to the fish, not something strange attached to a line. (See Figure 20.)

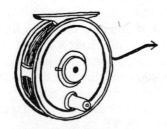

Figure 18. FLY REEL

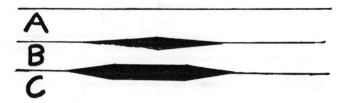

Figure 19. FLY LINES

These are the three types of fly line: level, double-tapered, and weight-forward "bullet" or "fast-taper."

A. The level line is used mainly for medium and short casts with a six-foot leader and weightless or weighted hook for bait or flies.
B. This is the double taper: a flat running line, a taper to a designated thickness, and a tapering off again toward the end with a short length of level line before the leader. Tapered lines of from six to nine feet are used for wet and dry fly-fishing. Forty- to fifty-foot casts are made with the average rod when using light flies or very small bait.
C. This is the weight-forward taper. It is used for long-distance work using small flies or a single fly. The reason this type of line is recommended is that the long running line behind the taper remains on the reel while you are false-casting to gain power in the cast. A very short and quick taper, this is the only part of the line that is in the air during the preparatory false cast. The weight will carry the running line out.

The variations in all these lines for specific weights of rod are shown in the rod and line recommendations.

There are two basic types of fly lines, the *floating* and the *sinking*.

The floating is used for most fly-fishing when it is desirable for the line to float, and the sinking is for wet deep-water fly-fishing.

The American Fishing Tackle Manufacturers' Association (AFTMA) designations and alphabetical designations are:

In the weight-forward lines (30 yards long):

FLOATING	SINKING
GAAF-9	GAF-8
GAF-8	GBF-7
GFB-7	HCF-6
HCF-6	HDG-5
HDG-5	

In the double taper (30 yards long):

FLOATING	SINKING
GBG-7	GBG-7
HCH-6	HCH-6
HDH-5	HDH-5
HEH-4	HEH-4

In the level lines (25 yards long):

FLOATING	SINKING
B-7	B-7
C-6	C-6
D-5	D-5
E-4	E-4
F-3	

Figure 20. LEADERS FOR FLY-FISHING

Leaders used to be made from gut, but now nylon is the best material.
Leaders come in all pound tests from 7X small to 1X large, and the pound
test is from about a half pound to ten pounds. There are both level and
tapered leaders. The tapered leaders are made from stepped-down sections of leader tied together, or you can buy nylon tapered leaders that
are manufactured or "drawn" in specific tapers. If it is desired to taper a
drawn leader further "up" or "down," sections can be added by tying the
desired strands together.

One manufacturer's sample lists the tapered leaders as follows:

SIZE	TEST
6X	2-lb.
5X	3-lb.
4X	4-lb.
3X	5-lb.
2X	6-lb.
1X	7-lb.
0X	8-lb.

Fly-rod action is important when balancing fly-fishing tackle
for casting. The combinations in the "ROD-REEL-LINE-LEADER-
FLY" table offer good general guidelines to cover basic needs.
The heavier combination is used frequently in salmon and bass
fishing when extra distance is needed, as in a stiff wind, and
where heavy flies are in order. All actions specified in the chart
are medium. The stiff-action rods are preferred if the angler is
going to do a great deal of extra-long-cast dry fly-fishing. (See Figure 21.)

ASSEMBLING THE TACKLE

To assemble the gear, place the fly reel on the rod handle so
the reel faces down and the line on the reel coils off from the bottom of the reel toward the first line guide. Secure the reel well. If
the rod handle has two rings, press them in against the reel foot

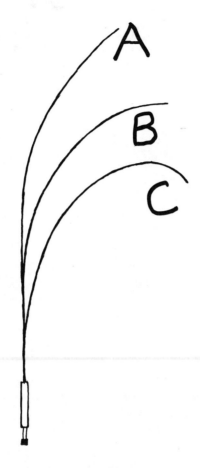

Figure 21. FLY-ROD ACTIONS
Shown are three types of fly-rod action, referred to in the text as stiff (dry fly), medium, and soft action.

A. The stiff is for very snappy false casting of a long line and the casting of a dry fly. In the case of the bass-bug rod, specifically designed to throw the heavier, wind-resistant bugs, a long, nine-and-a-half-footer is needed in this action. Some stiff-action dry fly rods are only six feet long.
B. The medium-action rod is for both shorter-length dry fly casting and wet fly-fishing with one or two flies.
C. The soft-action rod is for shorter dry fly fishing, wet-fly, nymph fishing, and very light baits. Tapered lines to fit are shown in the table of recommendations for balanced tackle. If the line does not fit the rod it will not cast well, so balanced rod and line is a must.

Rod-Reel-Line-Leader-Fly Table

FISHING TYPE	ROD LENGTH (medium action)	REEL	LINE TAPER	LEADER SIZE	FLY SIZE
Panfish, small trout and bass	7–7½ ft.	Small	HDH	Taper to 4X (Taper to 5X)	12, 14 (14, 16)
Medium trout, bass longer casts	8–8½ ft.	Medium	HCH	Taper to 3X	10, 12, 14
Heavy trout and bass	9 ft.	Large	GAF	Taper to 3X or 2X	8, 10, 12
Bass bug, salmon	9½–10 ft.	Large	G2AF	Taper to 2X	4, 6, 8, 10

tightly. If a screw-locking reel seat is present on your rod, secure the reel firmly in place. Thread the line out from the reel and through the first rod guide. Now insert the second section of the rod, lining up the guides before you insert so as not to twist the ferrule joints. Thread the line through these guides to the next section or tip. With the line extending from the rod tip, attach the leader loop with the line-to-leader knot as shown in the chapter on terminal tackle.

It is best to start fly casting without using a fly. Practice this over water or over a snag-free lawn. Do not cast the line over sand, concrete, or gravel, since the line finish is not made to stand friction and roughness.

ROD GRIP

The handle of the fly rod is ahead of the reel (see Figures 17 and 22). Your rod grip has nothing to do with the reel. You cast the rod with the right hand. The reel is tended with the left hand. The main pressure point in the cast, particularly the forward part of the cast, is the thumb, which exerts the pressure. With

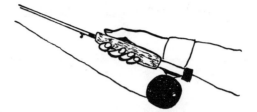

Figure 22. FLY-ROD GRIP
The manner in which the fly rod is grasped is with the thumb resting
comfortably on the top of the rod and in a direct line with the wrist. The
thumb is the pressure point on the forward casting action to transfer the
pressure to your wrist.

the thumb on top, the wrist will not have the tendency to break,
which would allow the rod to swing too far back from the vertical position at the peak of the cast.

Again, do not grasp the rod handle too tightly. Be relaxed
about it or you will tend to tense up and tire quickly.

THE CAST

Fly casting isn't the easiest type of casting, but it needn't be
hard to master. Armed with the correct initial steps the angler
soon learns to ad lib according to his own needs. Remember, the
main secret is that the line must travel straight out behind you on
the backcast and be allowed to extend almost to its full length
before you make the move to bring it forward. This will make
more sense to you as you begin to study the diagrams and practice and get the feel of the casting motion. But it's so important
I'm going to repeat it. *You must learn to wait on the backcast for
your line and leader to extend almost fully behind the rod tip before
you bring the rod forward into the forecast.*

I suggest you study the following description of the cast in conjunction with Figure 23. Read it through and then try it with
your rod. Then read it again and practice again with your rod.
Start yourself off with about twenty feet of line and leader.

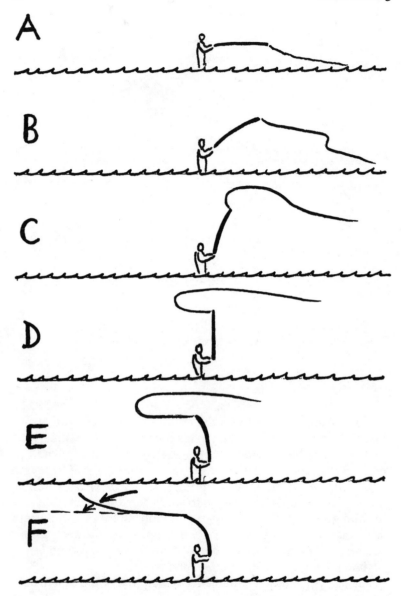

Figure 23. BASIC CASTING STEPS

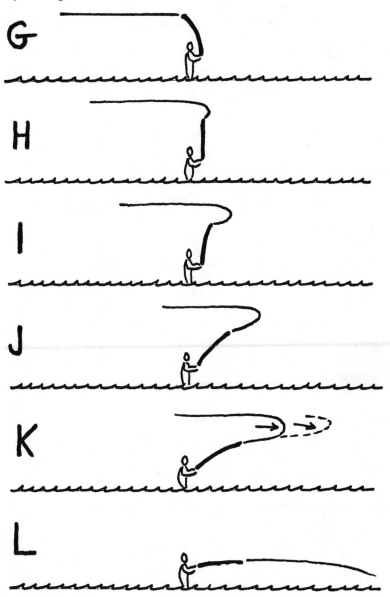

Figure 23. BASIC CASTING STEPS (Cont.)

Notice that as in spin and bait casting the entire casting motion is conducted by the hand and wrist. The wrist is the fulcrum of power and directs all energy which is transferred to the rod. In this casting the rod does practically all the work for you. Allow the rod to perform its function *for* you, since all you need to do is guide it and apply pressure as needed.

Starting at the pickup (A) in Figure 23, and moving to B, you exert an upward snaplike pressure. At C your effort stops for a split second and the rod does all the performing, bending as shown in a backward direction (D, E). This timing allows the line to sail out behind and above you (F).

Do not let your casting hand flip over backward past the vertical. If you do your rod will go too far back, lose its power, and the line will fall too low.

The instant your line straightens out behind you (actually a split-split-second *before* it has completely straightened out—but forget this for now), you pressure forward sharply into the forecast. (Sharply. Not jerkily or abruptly. The fly cast is a collection of different motions all blended together into one smooth motion.) The forward part of the cast is quite similar to the backward part, or backcast.

Try falsecasting a bit. This involves letting your line extend out in front of you on the forecast but not letting it drop to position A and instead sweeping it back again into a backcast, then a forecast, then a backcast, without stopping and without the line ever lowering.

To complete a forward cast simply follow through on the forecast into positions H and I (at which point again, as in the backcast, your casting hand pauses a moment and lets the forward whip of the rod do the work of throwing out the line for you— J, K), and if you're casting properly your line should unfurl out smoothly in a straight line before you onto the grass or water.

Note again that both arm and forearm are virtually stationary throughout. Your hand and wrist and the rod itself do the work.

To lengthen your cast you want to use your left (line) hand to control the amount of line you have out. (Use a double-tapered line. For now the HDH double-tapered line on a medium-action rod of seven-and-a-half feet will give you the basics.)

Before casting, grasp the line (with your left hand of course) between the reel and the first line guide. Begin the cast by lifting the line off the water, and with your left hand pull – or strip – off a few feet of line from the reel, making the backcast as usual.

On the forward throw you release the line that you stripped from the reel. The forward whip of the rod throws the line out and it slips through the fingers of your left hand, which takes hold of it again once it has stopped.

Now make the backcast again and notice that the additional line you have out causes additional pressure. A slightly longer pause is necessary now at the top (to allow the longer line time to straighten out behind you), and a slightly more powerful forward motion is required (since the added line makes the overall amount of line you have out heavier, and readier to drop). Also, by the same token, you'll have to make a slightly more powerful move when you pick the longer line up off the water in the first place.

Now strip off another couple of feet of line as before. As you draw back for the next false cast, strip off line from the reel, and as you push forward release the line through your fingers, still keeping control. As the line straightens out, pull back before it begins to drop, using a bit more power. Strip off more line now as it is coming back and on the forward throw allow that extra line to slip through your left hand's fingers. By now you should be falsecasting nearly thirty feet of line evenly in the air.

Stay relaxed. Don't make any jerky motions, even when pausing at the top or flicking the rod forward or whipping it back. The fly cast is one smooth motion. And you don't have to put that much muscle into it. It's all a matter of timing and practice. Don't expect to pick it up the first time you try either. It's harder than spin-casting and bait-casting. But once you begin to get the feel of it you'll find it relatively easy.

Keep your casting hand, wrist, forearm, and arm *relaxed*. Sometimes when beginners are experiencing trouble their casting arm tends to tense up to try and correct what's wrong, but this only makes it worse. *Relax* your casting arm and wrist, while at the same time keeping every thing firm and smooth and decisive – and keep trying. You'll find it a wonderful sensation when the feel of the basic fore-and-aft fly cast first dawns on you.

Another common mistake is to get the falsecasting routine down, and then panic on the real cast.

When you're ready to let your line unfurl out forward and down on the water just make the forward cast basically as if you were falsecasting and your line should unfurl smoothly out straight on the water before you.

Essentially, that's all there is to the basic fly cast. Refinement comes later.

Let's start again.

It is not advisable to try and lift all that line you've got out, so you have to strip in some line. Hold the rod at about two o'clock and grasping the line near the first line guide strip in by pulling in line (three times and about two feet each time), coiling the line in loops in your left hand.

Now reach up and back with the rod tip and lift the line off the water to begin falsecasting again, swinging the rod to the vertical position. Continue this forward and back falsecasting action just as you did before. When your line is flowing in the air back and forth easily, you can again lengthen the line, adjusting the timing and pressure of the cast and extending the line even farther than you did the last time.

Note that a slower back-and-forth motion is needed as the line extends out and more pressure is needed to keep the line up off the water.

Let it down again on the forecast. Don't force it. You want that leader to fall on the water with hardly a ripple.

VARIATIONS ON THE FORE-AND-AFT CAST

Some variations are worth noting at this early stage in your casting. If you wish to change the direction of a cast, you can do so during the falsecast by gradually changing your point of aim more toward the left or right. Or you can make the cast with your rod at a slight angle away from the vertical, leaning the rod left or right as your choice dictates.

The basic cast can be made horizontally over the water, or sidearm. This is tricky however, since because you have so little space to drop down to the water the speed of the cast must be much faster. This cast is used when casting to a target under overhanging branches or when casting into a stiff wind.

If you are casting to a rock above you in the stream and you wish to cast with a bend in the leader section, either to the left or the right, turn your hand in the direction needed on the forward throw and then, just before the line touches the water on the drop, come up sharply about ten degrees with the rod. This hand-roll will whip the end of the leader in the desired direction.

SHOOTING THE LINE

In this case you are armed with a powerful and long fly rod with a stiff tip section and a weight-forward tapered line. Since all the weight of the line is located in the first few yards, it is difficult to make the usual falsecast.

In order to build up casting power in the rod, wave it back and forth and make a short falsecast with only about half the taper out from the rod tip. This heavy weight in the air, being pushed back and forth by the stiff rod, will build up the rod tension needed to shoot the line forward. The cast is begun the same as the fore-and-aft falsecast. Strip off several coils of line. (At first you might drop the line at your feet for practice.) When you choose to release the line for the forward drop, the weight of the line combined with the power of the cast will rapidly pick up all that line and even strain the reel for more. So give it more!

Strip off more line for the next cast. You'll find, when you learn the tricky timing, that you can shoot as much as thirty feet of line. Add this to the thirty feet of line already in the air and you are reaching out almost to the sixty-foot mark. That little dry fly on the end is really going for a ride.

To help the cast further and give it more power, you perform what is known as the *power cast* or *double haul*. As you begin the pickup off the water, or the backward swing from the front falsecast position, grasp the line near the first line guide and pull it in with a sharp downward pull. As the line flies backward to the back position of the falsecast, release the line you have taken in. Then as it begins to fly forward, pull line in again from the first guide and release it. In this way you are amplifying the power of the rod through the restriction of the line during the cast.

LINE RETRIEVE IN UPSTREAM FISHING

Upstream fishing against the current requires a constant retrieve of the line with the left hand while you are casting with the right. Right after the upstream cast is made, begin to strip line in. Don't pull it in too fast or you'll pull the fly that is supposed to drift by itself down to you. In stripping the line on a fairly short cast, allow the slack line to slip through your fingers and drift below. On very long casts, coil the line in your hand. You will be needing it to feed out from the reel again as in your first steps. You no longer deal with the reel but handle the line that is floating behind you or coiled in your hand. For all intents and purposes, *you* are now the reel.

Across-stream and across-and-downstream fishing is not as difficult as direct upstream fishing. The line can be allowed to float below you without tangling. But if you are using a very long line, again you should coil it in your hand and feed it out on the cast.

And remember, when you're shortening your line your left hand reaches up close to the first line guide to take hold of the line and pull in. This way you make your coils automatically.

ROLL CAST

This cast is fully as important as the fore-and-aft cast. It is used when there is no room for the backswing of the conventional cast. If you are fishing with brush and trees or a bridge or cliff behind you, you cannot perform the usual cast so you use the roll cast.

At other times you do not need to bother with the conventional cast – for instance when you are fishing down- and across-stream and wish only to whip the flies out into the current a short distance.

You'll find hundreds of instances where you'll use the roll cast rather than the fore-and-aft.

Note: In learning and practicing the roll cast don't expect to be able to do it on a lawn. You need a pond or swimming pool, because the sliding-over-the-water action of your line won't work unless the line is lying on a relatively frictionless surface.

The following description refers to Figure 24.

Starting with your line out before you in the in-stream position (A), whip your rod back up to the vertical in one quick move (B, C). You are not lifting your line off the water here. You are sliding it back over the water toward you. As your rod and line assume the position shown in C, you are ready to make the forward-pressure move that will result in the wide, high, loop pattern shown in G, H, and I.

Now, at position C the forward pressure is exerted toward positions D and E. The line continues to pass near your face on its upward swing to form the loop which begins to develop as you bring down the rod to position F. When your rod comes down to position G the line is now on its way out toward the target (H, I, J, K), and at L the line's end falls in the target area. The whole thing is really a snap (pun intended!) Snap back up and then down again and the whole routine performs by itself. As you can see in Figure 24, after position G is reached only the line is working—not you.

Once again now. Start with the line out, bring the rod up sharply to the vertical and just as sharply down again. The line reacts by coming close to you and forming a loop to straighten out in the air above the target and then fall to the water.

Fascinating to watch, fun to perform. You'll use this cast a great deal, in your stream fishing especially.

As usual, try the cast with a short line at first to get the routines set in your head. When you want to extend the line on this cast, all you do is strip some line from the reel preparatory to the cast and then feed it out at position G. To add more power and zip to the cast, as you begin the pickup strip in line from the first guide and pull down on the line hard as you move to the vertical position.

Note: The roll cast is not difficult once learned, but the feel of it can sometimes be a trifle hard to pick up. If you're having troubles, try bringing your rod back from A through B to C *slowly*. Pause at C to see if everything is in order, and then go ahead and initiate the forward, downward thrust. Keep trying it this way until your line acts as depicted in G through L. Then you can start the quick one-move take-back as originally described.

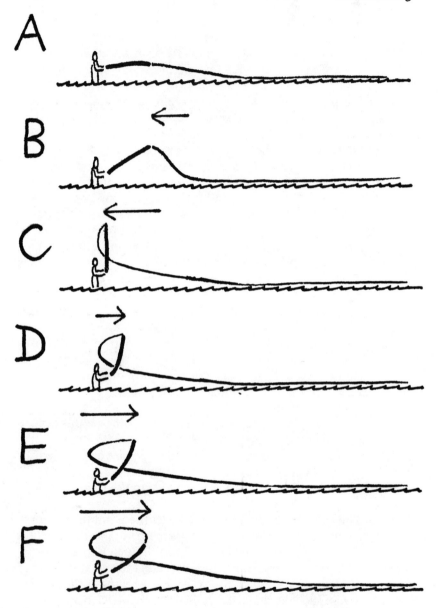

Figure 24. THE ROLL CAST

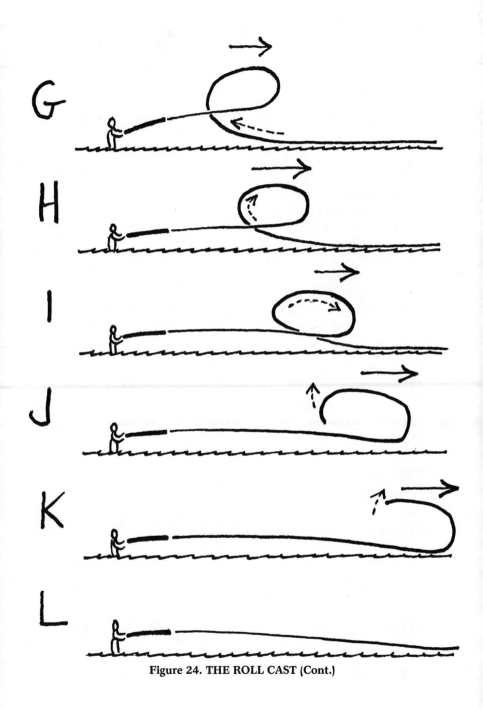

Figure 24. THE ROLL CAST (Cont.)

ROLL-PICKUP CAST

This is seldom performed by the average angler, yet it is a very simple and necessary part of casting.

Begin an ordinary pickup as you would for the conventional fore-and-aft cast. After you have started the pickup you very forcefully snap the rod forward and down again, which pulls the fly and end of the leader off the water. Almost as quickly as you did the first two moves (and as the fly leaves the water), pull back harder than usual on the regular backcast and then begin your conventional falsecast forward.

Now go through this again. The line and fly are on the water. Snap a sharp pickup motion and at the same time snap the rod down again. As the fly comes out as a result of this action on the line, pull back hard and perform your regular falsecast.

Note how little water disturbance you caused. Just for contrast, put your line and fly out there on the water again and in one motion begin to pull it all back to start the regular cast. See what a strip of water is disturbed?

In order to get more power in this roll pickup—especially when fishing upstream against a current dragging the fly down toward you—strip in line at the instant you begin the pickup and forward flip. This will make sure the line will act as it should in preparation for the falsecast position.

STRIKING, PLAYING, AND LANDING

In fly casting, the left (line) arm controls the line flow. The fish is not played from the reel as it is in spinning and bait-casting. The line arm (except when playing big steelhead or Atlantic salmon) does all the controlling in conjunction with the rod pressure that is exerted by the rod hand pulling the rod back against the pull of the fish.

If the fish strikes when there is little or no slack line on the water (or hanging loosely underwater) the strike will be felt immediately. Your reaction must not be too abrupt or strong. Actually, when this occurs, the fish usually hooks himself! It is when the line is slack that more attention must be paid to taking up that slack at the instant the fish hits. If there is too much slack he'll have time to reject the fly in one quick split second, so try to control your slack line as much as possible.

At the time of landing your fish, the rod is held high. The slack line is gathered in the left hand. At convenient times during the fight, as the line is brought in, the line can be held in the rod hand while the left hand is used in reeling in slack.

To net the fish, be sure that it is fully played out. If you are fishing from a wading position in a fast stream, try to get the fish upcurrent from you and then let it drop back slowly into the submerged landing net. Hold the line in the rod hand and execute the landing with the left hand, free now since the line is under control. Don't swipe at the fish, but rather merely bring the net into a position where the fish will drop back into it and then you can scoop it up, relaxing the line in the rod hand at that same instant to release the pressure from the bent rod.

5

Terminal Tackle

ARTIFICIAL FLIES FALL into two basic categories: those made to imitate insects and those made to look like minnows or small bait fish.

They are made of feathers and bits of hair or fur tied onto a hook shank covered with a "body." Some are designed to float like an insect on the water surface. Others are fished below the surface.

Various trout fly types are illustrated in Figure 25.

The minnow and bait-fish imitations called streamers and bucktails are fished underwater, and some are weighted to make them sink even deeper. They are made in various sizes and shapes and are cast only with the fly rod. (The one exception is when using plastic bubble and light spinning gear.)

A special type of fly is called the bass bug, the large fluffy lure too light for bait or spin casting but just right for specially designed, heavier fly rods. Bass bugs imitate big bugs, moths, mice, frogs, and the like. They float when cast and are popped and

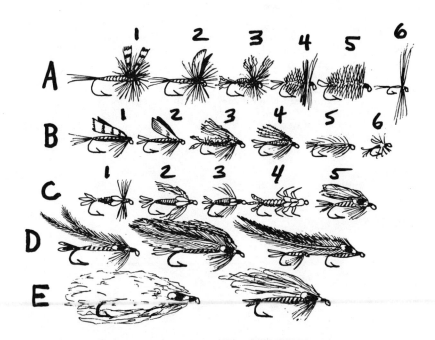

Figure 25. TROUT FLY TYPES

These are the various types of flies used for trout, panfish, and bass fishing in fresh water with fly-fishing tackle.

ROW A shows the dry-fly types. These flies are made to imitate mayflies, caddis flies, stone flies, and aquatic insects that hatch into their flying stage in the stream and in lakes. They are made to float on the surface.

Row A (left to right):
1. Divided wing type made from fibers of duck side feathers.
2. Divided wing type with sections of duck wing feathers paired to flare out.
3. Typical hair-wing fly or Wulff heavy-hook pattern particularly good for night trout fishing and Atlantic salmon fishing. It is also used for bass fishing.
4. This is the bivisible. Strands of white hackle are tied in ahead of the basic fly to make it more visible in poor light.
5. The Palmer-tied fly with the hackle tied in all the way to the hook bend. These flies sometimes have short wings as well.
6. The dainty spider fly tied on an 18 or 20 size hook. Note the long hackles.

ROW B (left to right):
1. Wet version of A, 1.
2. Wet version of A, 2.
3. Wet version of A, 3.
4. Sparsely dressed hackled fly with soft hackles so the fly will sink, not float.
5. Wet-style Palmer-like fly.
6. The wet version of the midge or spider fly.

ROW C (left to right):
1. Pattern of standard mayfly nymph with wing cases.
2. Longer, heavier stone-fly pattern.
3. General type of nymphlike fly.
4. Hard-bodied, exact-imitation type of plastic-molded variety.
5. Bucktail-like combination wet-nymph fly.

ROWS D AND E
Bucktails and streamers.

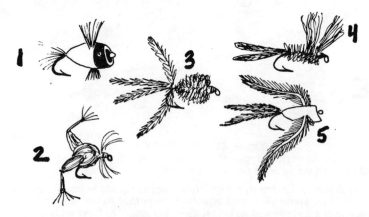

Figure 26. BASS BUGS
Bass bugs are special creations for use with the heavy fly rod and forward-tapered line. They represent moths, bugs, beetles, frogs, mice, or anything small or fluttering on the water surface that might look like something the bass would like to eat.

1. The wooden-bodied hair bug.
2. Entire bug made of hairs (usually deer) with long feather fiber wings.
3. Hair-bodied bug with streamer feathers.
4. Cork-, plastic- or wooden-body bug with streamer feathers.
5. Frog or mouse imitation made of long deer body hairs tied to resemble either a frog or mouse.

These lures are made to float on the surface and be popped by rod-tip action and line manipulation.

kicked across the surface of the water in a lifelike motion that attracts the fish. They are used mainly in bass fishing, although they are also quite effective on large trout at night. (See Figure 26.)

PLASTIC WORMS AND EELS, ARTIFICIAL PORK CHUNK AND RIND

The plastic worm and the plastic eel have all but replaced the live variety that you take from the ground. They have a lifelike feel, action, and color and really do the job (see Figure 27). Frogs, bugs, mice, and a myriad of other fish foods have been aptly imitated in plastic and look lifelike enough to be frightening. They work!

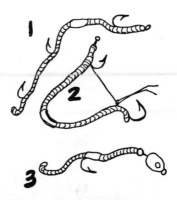

Figure 27. PLASTIC WORMS
Available at the tackle counter in a number of basic forms. Some are available without hooks so that you can insert your own ideas for particular needs.

1. A most deadly combination, mounted with three hooks. It is either a tied-on rig or the leader is inserted into the worm and the hooks tied into the leader and reinserted into the worm. A good rig for casting and still fishing.
2. The worm mounted on a weedless hook and attached so that the largest portion of the worm is free.
3. The metal jig with attached hook. The plastic worm is impaled on it or tied onto the hook, for deep-water fishing and also for casting with a fairly fast retrieve, bounced over the bottom and through the grass.

Rubber and plastic fluttering strips which resemble pork rind are also big sellers at the tackle stores. The fish like them and so do the fishermen because they eliminate the mess of handling and preserving the real thing and work as well or better. (See Figure 28.)

SPINNERS AND SPOONS

One day, legend tells us, a creative fisherman cut the bowl of a spoon from its handle, attached a hook at one end and some line at the other, and cast the contraption at a fish. When the angler retrieved the lure it wobbled in the water enticingly and the fish struck it. From that day on spoons in various forms, shapes, sizes, and colors have been important to fishing.

The heavier spoons are used with bait-casting rigs, the lighter ones with spinning gear and the very lightest with ultralight spinning and fly tackle.

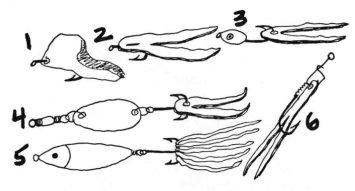

Figure 28. PORK RIND AND PORK CHUNK LURES
Bass and trout like meat and so fishermen have devised ways of cutting up bits and pieces of pork (easily available and, in the rind, practical since it holds the hook well) for bait. Here are a few of the types of cut for casting and trolling:

1. Pork chunk on hook.
2. Two-tail pork rind on hook.
3. Same as 2, on a weighted jig.
4. Strip pork on spoon (or spinner).
5. Thin rubber (pork strips) on sinking plug.
6. Strip-bait rig on special frame.

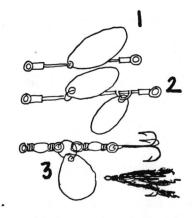

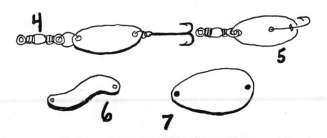

Figure 29. SPINNERS AND SPOONS

Here are a few of the many variations of spinners and spoons. They are used for ultralight spinning and fly-rod work, formal spinning, and bait casting and trolling. Sometimes as many as ten spinners are employed in deep-trolling spoon-spinner rigs. Spinners are often mounted ahead of a spoon, which can be tops in deep trolling gear.

1. The single-bladed Indiana.
2. The double Indiana. In each case the line is attached to one end, the hook or leader and hook to the other.
3. The famous Colorado Spinner with the blade revolving between two swivels. It is one of the most deadly and can be used in all types of terminal tackle and fishing gear.
4. The typical spoon rig, preceded here by the swivel and with the treble hook attached. Feathered hooks can also be used here as with others.
5. The Johnson solid-mounted-hook spoon for trolling and casting. Good with worm bait.
6, 7. The original spoons just as they were made from a real spoon and handle. They can be mounted in all ways and used under all fishing conditions.

Spinners are merely spoons hung on a shaft that revolves instead of wobbling, giving a different effect in the water, although just as deadly. They too come in many sizes and designs. Some spinner combinations have from two to six blades revolving on one piece of terminal tackle. These are used for trolling. Figure 29 shows some varieties of spoons and spinners.

PLUGS

The term *plug* has an unknown origin. Perhaps it was a plug from a barrel with a hook attached to it that was first cast to a fish. The early inventors of plugs carved fishlike shapes from sections of broom handles, painted them, and attached singles and later treble hooks to them. These were cast on a silk line via a bait-casting rod and reel. In more recent times most of the wooden plugs have been made of plastic and further refined and balanced for all kinds of actions in the water. They are beautifully painted to represent a variety of bait fish, frogs, and mice. Spinners and fins are attached for more action and attraction. Some have fluttery skirts and feathers tied on the hooks. Plugs come in all the sizes to be used with heavy tackle as well as with the smallest of the ultralight spinning gear. Some very small plugs can be cast with the fly rod.

Plug actions fall into definite categories as is shown in Figure 30. A broad selection of the illustrated types completes a basic collection of plugs.

NATURAL BAITS

There are quite a few natural baits (see Figure 31) that all game fish feed on, and they are found, naturally, in the vicinity of the specific fish that eat them. The only "stranger" to the crowd is the earthworm, which finds its way to the stream or lake when the rain washes it in or it drifts down as a wash-in into a stream that enters a lake. Yet the earthworm is the universal first choice of all freshwater fish. If you have never fished with anything else, you could enjoy a lifetime of success on all game fish, using only the earthworm.

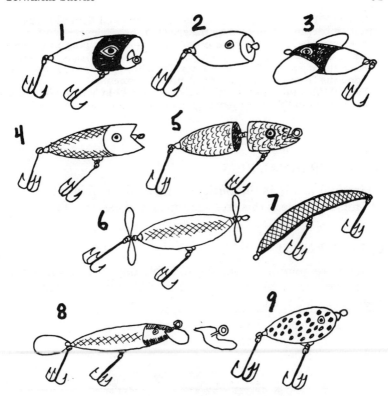

Figure 30. PLUGS
Some of the countless shapes and forms of floating-popping, floating-diving, sinking-diving, and sinking plugs. They come in all colors, particularly natural colors of bait fish such as the creek chub and yellow perch.
Some come with red heads, green heads, or black heads—and frog and
minnow scales that look like the real thing.

1. The typical popping plug that floats when at rest.
2. The smaller version for spinning and lighter tackle work.
3. The popular jitterbug popping plug that comes in big sizes for heavy
   tackle and in several weights down to ultralight spinning size. These
   are all surface-acting plugs.
4. A typical surface-floating plug, but one that dives and zigzags the
   faster you pull it.
5. Same as 4, but jointed. Most of the other plugs are also available
   jointed.
6. One of the favorites, known as the fore-and-aft spinner plug, which
   comes in either floating or sinking weight. It is drawn across the sur-

face or, in the sinking version, allowed to sink and then be retrieved with its depth determined by the speed of the retrieve.
7. The wounded-minnow type of rolling, zig-zagging plug that floats when at rest.
8. Basic sinking plug. Dives deep according to the speed of your retrieve. Bend the front fin as shown for depth adjustment.
9. Basic sinking plug. Just a plain heavy, with built-in action. The action is triggered in this lure by rod-tip action and line-retrieve speed.

BASIC TERMINAL RIGS

Terminal tackle is the business end of the tackle setup. The variants available in this area are almost endless. (See Figure 32.)

USEFUL KNOTS

There are countless fisherman's knots that have been developed over the years. The ones shown here are the necessary ones. (See Figure 33.)

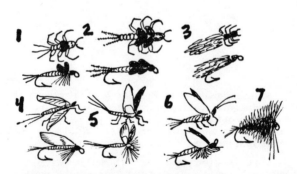

Figure 31. STREAM INSECTS AND THEIR ARTIFICIAL IMITATIONS
1. Typical mayfly nymph and, below, its nymphal imitation.
2. Stone-fly nymph and, below, its imitation.
3. The caddis-fly nymph in its case of bark and, below, gravel-sand.
4. Dead and floating mayfly. Below this is a typical mayfly pattern.
5. Floating and very live mayfly dun and, below, the classical dry fly.
6. Caddis and stone flies wear their wings angled back, and the imitation is tied likewise.
7. The fly that seems to imitate them all: the bivisible.

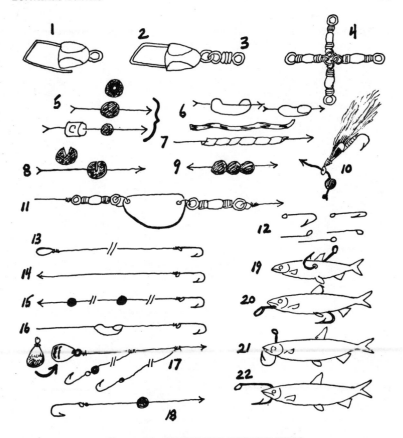

Figure 32. TERMINAL TACKLE RIGS

Shown here are the many ways of assembling your terminal tackle that you will find necessary in all types of freshwater fishing. There are countless variations and combinations of all these "ties" and "makes," but shown here are all you need to know, at least at first. Buy all the parts and then sit down and assemble them, keeping in mind what each will be used for.

1. The snap. This is used in bait casting and spinning when tied from line to leader, line, or metal leader to which you snap on a lure or hook or rig. It is shown open and . . .
2. Closed. (Looks like a safety pin!)
3. The snap-swivel. This combination cuts out the twist of the lure or rig that might be caused in the casting or trolling of the terminal lure.
4. The four-way swivel combination. It can be made in a three-way rig also. It is used with hooks and weights for still fishing or slow trolling. The bottom spoke can, for example, tie into the sinker.

5. This is the heavy slip sinker with the hole in the middle. It is used as a cast weight with the line flowing through it freely. The baited hook can be taken by the fish without any noticeable drag. He can run with the bait without being scared by the pull of the lead. When he has run a bit, you can then set the hook! The drawing with the C is a cork attached well ahead of the line to help keep it off the bottom. It too has a hole big enough for the line to flow through smoothly.

6. The clamp-on type sinker. A bit heavier than the wraparound lead or BB-shot lead. Clamps on as shown and can be more easily removed than the split-shot BB.

7. The lead strip wraparound that can be lengthened or shortened at will for just the correct weight to solve the problem of the moment. Knots can be tied ahead and behind to keep it from slipping on the line.

8. The BB split shot. Place the line in the slot and close the lead tight.

9. Several split shots can be clamped on at intervals. This is good for fly-rod or light-spinning casting of a weighted fly or bait.

10. The split shot shown ahead of a streamer fly. Note that the end of the leader is knotted so that the lead will not slip off. A very effective way to weight a fly.

11. The trolling fin. This is attached to the running line from the swivel, and the swivel behind is attached to the terminal tackle, weights, and bait hooks.

12. The offset bend hook, the straight hook, the turned-up eye hook, the turned-down eye hook, and the straight eye hook. These are the basic hook eye types and their choice is really a matter of personal preference.

13. The leader loop and attached hook. These can be bought this way, or you can tie them this way yourself. Also, there is a metal leader encased in plastic for use in bass, pike, and muskie fishing.

14. The hook is tied into a strip of leader material or directly to the line.

15. Split shot clamped on at intervals for easy casting.

16. The clamp-on weight shown on the leader.

17. The plumb-shaped weight is attached to the line at the end with the two bait hooks tied in at convenient intervals up the main line.

18. Split shot attached to the hook and leader/line.

19. Live minnow hooked for still fishing.

20. Hooked through the belly with hook protruding through the belly.

21. Hooked through the head for trolling or casting or still fishing.

22. Hooked through the head with the shank forward for casting and trolling.

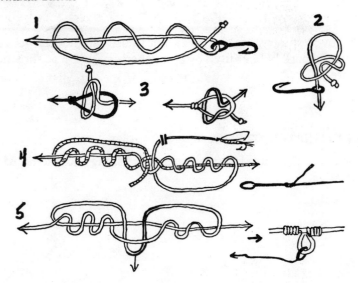

Figure 33. KNOTS

1. The simple clinch knot is good for quick tying on of the hook or lure to the line or leader. Put on a couple or more rolls to be sure, if you like, and for additional safety you can also double the end back into the wide loop at the bottom.
2. The ancient turle knot is a good one for tying the leader onto the hook.
3. These are two variations of a simple way of securing the looped leader to the fly line.
4. This is a simple way to create a loop for a looped leader. When finished, merely pull the loop down and tighten the knot.
5. This is the line-to-leader knot, a way of joining two sections of leader together, especially if you desire to leave an end long for a tippet. (The two- or three-dropper or tippet leader is used in two- and three-fly wet-fly fishing. Or you can use two flies of dry pattern if you prefer.)

Learn to tie these knots. Learn to tie them in the dark. Once you can do this you'll never be at a loss!

PLASTIC BOBBER

If you're spincasting and you want to use the modern version of the old cork bobber used by still fishermen, use it as shown in Figure 34.

STEELHEAD BAIT RIG

A special rig is used in steelhead trout fishing and is detailed in Figure 35.

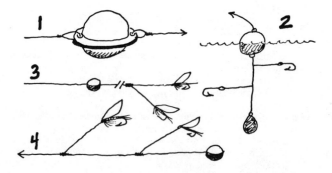

Figure 34. PLASTIC BUBBLE OR BOBBER
The plastic bubble or "bobber" and its use with spinning tackle. The old cork bobber has gone modern! Now you can cast even the daintiest of flies and small live baits by using the bobber—and still fishing, of course, is the natural use for the bobber, as it always has been.

The bobber can also be used with bait-casting gear and particularly with the fly rod, since it is so light. An effective use of the bobber is in conjunction with the fly rod and the closed-face spinning reel loaded with monofilament line. This can be cast great distances with ease.

1. Plastic bubble (can be weighted by adding water).
2. Conventional "above the bait" rig.
3. Ahead of flies.
4. Behind flies (best for long casts).

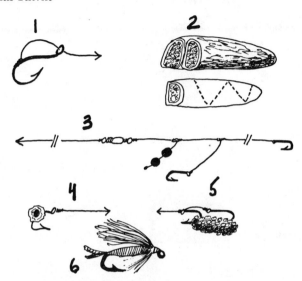

Figure 35. SPECIAL STEELHEAD TROUT RIGS
While the steelhead is a trout and can be caught by the same fishing methods as are used on the other trout species, the steelhead is a bit different from the others, and many special rigs are used in catching them.

1. Snell-knot egg hookup. This is made to hold a cluster of eggs or bits of yarn resembling salmon eggs. (Good for worms, too!)
2. Cut chunks of salmon eggs. These are hooked in various ways (as in 1 for instance) and drifted in the current during the salmon runs. The steelhead follow the salmon up the streams, feeding mainly on their discarded eggs and seldom taking flies or lures. *NOTE:* Egg clusters are cut from half skein of eggs for rig.
3. Weighted hook setup for drifting salmon-egg cluster.
4. Single egg on small salmon-egg hook.
5. Cluster eggs on two hooks.
6. Weighted streamer fly for use during the summer runs when the steelhead are not feeding exclusively on salmon eggs. Spinning lures, spoons, and spinners also work.

6

Tackle Repair and Care

CARE OF TACKLE requires only a minimum of mechanical ability. If you can work a simple screw, you can care for all your gear properly. All you need is a bit of patience and the desire to keep what you have in good order. Keep a can of good oil, some silicone, grease, a few old rags, some toothpicks, and the proper tools handy at all times and you are set.

Rust and wear are what tear tackle down. Keep your gear away from sand and grit, or, if your reel gets dirty, take it apart after your trip, clean it, and re-oil it.

Before you put it away for the season, clean your reel well, reoil it, and it will be all set for next year. It is best to check your reels after two or three trips or any kind of hard usage and keep them oiled and cleaned.

Fly lines should be washed often, even though you use grease dressing on them, for they pick up a lot of dirt from the water. Simply run the line out on the grass and using a dry piece of cloth gently squeeze your way along the entire length two or three times. Then bathe the line in a very weak solution of soap and rinse thoroughly. Let it dry, grease it, and then reel the line back onto its spool. The same goes for the braided level lines used in spinning and bait casting, except that they are not greased.

Your rod requires constant observation, because breaks in the finish, bends in the joints or ferrules, and chips or scratches in the line guides can wreck a good line in no time. Remember that the line goes through those guides with much pressure and speed. They must be dirt-free and also kept free from scratches that would snag the line. If they become scratched they should be replaced. You must learn very quickly not to let your rods bounce around in the trunk of the car or the bottom of the boat. Treat them with respect and they will return the favor.

You have already learned how to avoid twisting the ferrules and thus scratching the sides when setting up your tackle. Remember this and also remember to clean the ferrules each time before you assemble the rod to eliminate dust or grime or sand. Do not think that because the rod is made of glass that it is impervious to rot. It is not. When the surface becomes worn, clean it and then use spar varnish lightly. Put this on with the tips of your fingers and let it dry, not next to heat but in a dry place. To protect the finish of your rod, don't leave it out at night or baking all day in the sun. Wash it off after each use. Use wax a few times during the season to further protect it. This saves the messy bother of dressing down and revarnishing.

Keep hooks, swivels, sinkers, and the like in water-tight containers. It is also a good idea to keep your lures in containers, although this is not always easy. Store in boxes away from dew, spray, and bilge.

You'd be amazed at the lack of respect some anglers show their gear after they have spent much money on it. The tackle companies love those careless people!

Don't ever throw a rod away without removing the line guides and ferrules. You never know when those spares will come in handy. Keep them in the tackle box with some wax that can be melted to set them on the rod. Keep spare parts from old reels for temporary repair and save all screws. An on-location repair may demand using them to allow you to continue fishing.

7

Fishing Accessories

THESE ARE ITEMS of equipment other than the basic gear—terminal rigs and lures.

WATER TRANSPORTATION

Many times you can fish from the shore of a pond, lake, stream, or river. But when you can't, or prefer not to, some kind of water transportation is needed.

The canoe is one of the oldest forms of fishing craft. But just because America's great fishermen, the Indians, used it doesn't mean it is the best kind. A canoe is tippy and hard to handle in a wind. It is beautiful to use though when you're on a small lake or pond out of the wind, or when you can pick your time to fish and be sure the water is smooth and the wind is down. Paddling or drifting along you can approach good fishing spots with hardly a ripple and not disclose your presence to the fish. Learn not to bounce tackle and tackle boxes around in the bottom of the canoe for these vibrations will carry over into the fish's "ears" (the lateral line of sense organs shown in Figure 59). The same applies to tackle banging and paddle or oar rattling in all other kinds of craft.

The small rowboat, with or without a motor, is the most practical water transportation, for you can stand up in it to cast. But you must be careful, particularly if two of you are fishing together. If you are going any distance or intend to do a lot of trolling, a small outboard is a blessing, though again, try and keep its use to a minimum, approaching your fishing spot (for casting or still fishing) with the motor turned off.

It is best to row to the spot where you intend to fish.

Larger pleasure-type outboards with bigger motors are also recommended, but you should have a boat with high sides if you are fishing a big lake or broad river, since the wind can whip up quite dangerous waves. Use judgment in your ventures and do not go out in rough weather. The fish can wait and so can you. Also, be sure to leave the scene if a storm is seen approaching or if rain is obviously going to fall.

FOOTGEAR

If you are going to fish from the shore of a lake you'll need footgear designed to keep your feet warm and dry. Hip boots are the most practical for this, since they can be rolled down if you are not wading out into deep water. When you wish to wade, you can pull them up and attach them by the strap to your belt. Wear a pair of wool socks and fold your pant legs smoothly and comfortably so that there is little friction on your legs.

Hip boots can also be used for stream wading, although hip-deep wading is usually required and the added protection of hip or chest waders is advised. Good chest waders are quite expensive, so try and use the boots as much as possible. The chest waders are used when the angler is fly-fishing or spinning a big river or wishes to wade well out from the shore of a lake. When buying chest waders, or even hip waders, make sure you choose a loose fit, since a tight one will restrict leg motion greatly, and undue strain on the seams will cause them to part even before the first season has ended.

Waders are made in two styles: the boot foot, which is the

same as the rubber boot with the boot attached to the cloth top section, and the stocking foot, which requires wearing a pair of socks over the wader and then the addition of a pair of wading shoes. The former is preferred.

Both boot soles have additional aids in wading for different types of bottom. The ordinary boot soles suffice for most wading, but if you are wading in slimy streams or among clean slick rocks, a pair of felt attachments is recommended. When wading in gravel, rocks, and sand, a set of chains can be slipped on over the boot foot.

JACKETS

Fishing or wading jackets are made in two basic lengths, long and short. The long are for cold or windy weather when fishing from a boat or wading in shallow water. However, if you plan to wade in chest waders, a jacket of short length is advised, since the bottom of the long jacket would constantly be in the water, wetting the gear you keep in your pockets. Both jacket types have generous pockets for carrying lure boxes and accessories.

You should wear a hat, since you'll be out in the hot sunshine or in the cold wind. The visor type is recommended, because you'll have your eyes on the water and will need shade.

Polaroid glasses are an excellent addition, either in prescription if you wear glasses or just plain if you do not. Slip-on lenses are most impractical.

TACKLE BOX AND LURE CONTAINERS

You really should have three of these: one for your home stockpile, a second and large one for your boat, and a third for your car. Your basic stock should be large unless you like to make constant trips to the tackle store. Also, you may decide to fish at night after closing time at the store and must have what you need at hand. It is a good idea to buy a large supply of equipment, particularly lures, at the beginning of the season, so that you will never be caught short.

Terminal tackle should be kept apart in separate watertight compartments or containers (plastic for carrying, or glass if kept in the tackle box). Flies are filed neatly in special fly boxes. Dry flies are kept in boxes that are sectionalized so as not to crush the delicate fibers, and wet-fly boxes are used for the wets, nymphs, and streamers. Spinning lures should be kept in a box with slot sections or, preferably, in their own containers so that there is no danger of the hooks snagging or tangling.

Much of this is more easily understood at the tackle store. Present your case to the tackle salesman for his advice and also keep an eye on other anglers to see how they arrange their gear.

Tools such as small longnose pliers, small wrenches, various sizes of screwdriver, and additional screws and parts are good to have along in case of a streamside repair or a reel repair out on a lake. A small container of oil is helpful for additional lubrication. Small rags are also a necessity for quick cleaning needs.

WADING STAFF AND NETS

A wading staff can be made from an old ski pole (just cut the basket off) or an old broom handle (attach a leather strap to the top end and shave the other end to a point). When not in use, it can be attached to your belt.

For stream fishing, a short-handled net similar in size to a tennis racket is required and is attached to a stretch cord which in turn is snapped to the wading jacket. This is for use in landing the fish when you are wading.

A boat net is the same general shape as the wading net, but with a wider hoop and longer handle.

FISH KEEPERS AND BAIT BOXES

In order to keep your bait fish alive, a bait can is advised for boat fishing. It can be tied to a rope and lowered over the side. But remember to bring it aboard when you start the motor to move to another spot or go home!

Live bait for stream fishing is carried in a very small bait can attached to your belt and dipped into the water frequently so that the fish will not suffocate.

To keep your fish catch when fishing from a boat, a fish stringer, which contains a succession of very large safety-pin-type snaps, is recommended. The fish is attached by hooking the pin part through the lower jaw so that the fish can breathe freely in the water when the boat is stopped. In this way it is almost as if he were free. Also, remember to haul in the stringer when you are about to take off, and then keep the fish in the shade. If you have a cold box aboard it is better to kill the fish, clean them, and place the sections in the box.

The old-style bamboo fishing creel is worn by the stream angler to store his trout or bass, but many of the newer types of fishing jackets have air-vented creels on the back of the jacket with removable rubber linings so that the creel can be easily and frequently washed.

Insects are fish food, but also will use *you* for a meal. So take along insect repellant and keep it in your tackle box or pocket away from the lures and leaders.

A medicine kit is necessary in the car or boat, complete with a needle that has been sterilized and wrapped (for slivers or blisters), Band-Aids and bandage material, cotton and disinfectant such as Mercurochrome or Iodine—and don't forget the suntan lotion and aspirin.

Keep a small bottle of drinking water aboard the boat. Juicy fruits such as apples and oranges are also good insurance against thirst.

And don't forget your fishing license! Make sure this is in your wallet, or, if you are the ultra-careful type, leave your wallet in your car and carry the license in a waterproof container in your pocket. A copy of the fish laws is also good to have along just in case you have a problem remembering the length and catch limit.

Now let's go fishing!

8

Lake Fishing

FIRST WE'LL GET acquainted with lake conditions and some habits and characteristics of the more common kinds of lake fish. Then I'll take you out on the water and we'll do some fishing.

In many ways a lake is more difficult to read than a stream. On a stream, natural conditions dictate the fishing hot spots and the techniques for casting to the fish that are lying there. On a lake, such knowledge is not readily available.

But it can be uncovered in many ways.

One way, of course, is to employ a guide, especially in fishing a lake that is entirely unfamiliar to the angler. Another way is to look for a map of the lake and its hot spots—sometimes available. Even a simple road map of the territory usually details something of the lake shore, showing the inlets, outlets, tributary streams, major points of indentation, and importantly, ways of access by car or foot. Some also show boat landings, islands, and other features of interest to the fisherman. Often even better is a geodetic map of the area and this should be thoroughly studied and brought along on the trip, safely wrapped against water and spray. With the depths known in advance, it will be fairly simple to locate the possible hot spots.

Fish react to water temperature in the same fashion as humans do to air temperature. They move around in the lake, up and down and sideways, seeking a comfortable temperature. That's why they are found in some sections of a lake at one time and at another spot at another time. At some seasons they are found living and feeding on the surface and at others, hiding deep down. This has to be accepted and reckoned with.

Then there is the matter of feed. The gamefish will be where the food and baitfish are located. This circumstance can change by the hour. A sudden alteration in the climate conditions from rain today, hot to cold, or from cold to hot, or a serious drop or rise in the barometer can quickly and definitely alter all conditions. Merely casting hour after hour and traversing the shorelines, deeps, and shallows could be a waste of time regardless of the techniques used and mastery of tackle and gear.

In order for the angler not to completely miss the "luck" he deserves, or merely to bump into the good fishing on a few occasions during his possibly expensive stay at the lake, there are many constants upon which he can depend. In addition the guide, or the locals who will advise him from shore if he takes off in a boat alone to fish, know much of this information and can give it to him freely if he will listen.

The specific fish species must be known from study and accumulated past experience. Landlocked salmon and brook trout in the lakes of northern Maine and New Brunswick react to their homes in a much different way than the big largemouths of a Florida lake. The smallmouth bass of a Lake-of-the-Woods pond in Ontario don't live the same as those in Dale Hollow and the TVA lakes of Tennessee and Kentucky.

In order to enjoy excellent topwater casting and surface trolling for landlocked salmon, the angler has to be right on the spot just as the ice goes out from the lakes. There's a period then, when the smelt are running to their spawning streams and shore locations, when the landlocks can be taken in numbers by casting streamers and wet flies and even dry flies. But the minute the water surface warms up, they go deeper and deeper. In a matter of two weeks' time they can be taken from the top and then to a depth of ten feet or more. Same for the brook trout. Rainbow trout in the colder lakes in the northern states react somewhat the same, rising to flies in the first days and weeks of the season. Cutthroats in a Washington State lake may be found along the shoreline in early season but will quickly center in the deeper water leaving the shoreline to the bass for the remainder of the season. It is then a matter of trolling over the cooler spots, spring holes and stream entries—specific locations—rather than merely casing the lake by hours of fruitless casting and trolling.

Brown trout also react varyingly to weather conditions and water temperatures, although they can stand warmer water than brook or rainbow trout. They too have their day on the surface . . . then go down deep to join the lake trout in the cooler bands of water in a given lake.

Then there are various kinds of lakes—the shallow lakes and ponds and the deeper lakes and particularly the artificial impoundments and reservoirs. While these artificial lakes require a special kind of study, the fish react according to their needs.

A knowledge of the particular baitfish to be imitated is needed. Local guides and outfitters have spent many years in developing both standard flies and lures and special innovations that will catch fish under specific conditions on a specific lake or chain of lakes. Mark their advice and get those patterns. Also heed their recommended techniques for casting and trolling these flies.

In bass fishing, there is quite a bit of difference between the habits of smallmouth bass and largemouths in a given lake at specific times. The largemouth bass is more likely to put up with warmer temperatures and seek out warmer water. Usually the largemouth will be found in the shallower waters and along the lake shore in contrast to the smallmouth, particularly in the early part of the season. When the water gets too warm along the edges, even the largemouth will seek out the depths and join the smallmouth and lake trout.

Even during a twenty-four-hour period much movement can be charted for game fish, depending on the season, barometer, water temperature, and baitfish conditions.

LAKE FISH AND FAVORED TEMPERATURES

Regardless of everything else, the study of fish and their pre-ferred temperatures should be made. It has been, by excellent biologists and fisheries experts who depend on this knowledge to help them ascertain just what fish populations are best for the lakes and rivers under their supervision. This information together with actual fishing results can form a basis for ascer-taining just where and when to fish for specific varieties.

The panfish, such as bluegills, sunfish, crappies, and large-mouth bass, can stand temperatures of from 65 to 75 and even 80 degrees. Their lakes become much colder than this in the winter in northern zones. At these times they become very dormant, however. At the opposite end of the temperature spectrum are the lake trout and landlocked salmon. They survive best in tem-peratures of 40–55 degrees and are most active on the surface at this time. When the temperature of the lake rises above this point, they sink down to cooler levels. If it is colder such as in winter, they too become dormant. Yellow perch, smallmouth bass, pike, muskellunge, and pickerel like their homes warmed from 60 to 75 degrees for their most active period, while brown trout and rainbows like it a trifle cooler—somewhere between 45 to 50 up to 70 degrees. The brook trout likes it about ten degrees cooler for optimum action. Again, above and below these ranges the fish tend to be inactive or seek out new areas with more com-patible temperatures, sometimes moving down deep where fly fishing for them is not feasible.

In lakes in the northern states, temperatures range from near freezing on the bottom, depending on the depth, to a high of 80 degrees or more in exceptionally hot summer "dog days." The temperatures various species of fish prefer can tell the angler at just what depths to fish for them, or to forget trying to fish for them altogether with flies.

The only way to catch them in hot weather is very deep still-fishing.

UNDERSTANDING HOW A LAKE "WORKS"

In northern lakes where the temperatures vary over a wide

range, violent changes in the water take place. In winter, when the lake freezes over with ice, a kind of insulation covers the surface and the temperature ranges near freezing just under the "cap." Below this point, strangely enough, the water becomes warmer and more dense until a temperature of about 40 degrees is reached at the bottom. When the ice begins to deteriorate due to the longer period of sunlight reaching it as the spring advances, the ice begins to reach the point of breakup. This can happen in but a day or two and lo, the ice is "out." The lake is clear and breathing again – then comes the spring fishing action!

With the ice now gone from the lake the first phase of its annual change cycle takes place. The warmth from the sun raises the water temperature from near freezing to about 40 degrees. At this point the surface water matches the temperature of the warmer water that before was layered below the ice. Fish therefore come to the surface and range throughout the entire lake depths, since the water layers are nearly all the same. Fish that were dormant during the cold winter now feed with abandon in this period of spring activity.

Now, take into consideration the winds. That wind blowing over the lake should be blowing surface food to the shore, so it would be supposed that this shore ought to be the best to fish. But if the temperature of water along the on-wind shore is measured it will be found that the water is still too cold there for most fish. The opposite shore would be best because there the water would be a little warmer, a fact proven time and again by guides as well as biologists! So wind action can fool the angler. It can break up the ice prematurely, but it won't bring good fishing until the surface waters are at the proper temperatures.

As spring edges toward summer another change in the lake occurs. The surface water becomes increasingly warmer. This produces lighter water, lighter and warmer than that in layers below. A mixing of warm and cold water takes place forming a third layer of water which drops in temperature sometimes quite quickly. This middle layer can be a shallow band in a shallow lake or a wide band in deeper lakes. It remains at about the same general temperature all summer long and it is there that the fish will be found when the surface water gets too warm. At the same time there is little food deep down in a lake to lure fish there and the lowest water layer is often too cold, so it is not a truism that fishing is always best at the deepest part of the lake. It is better to work the intermediate zones all around the lake shore, the islands, mid-lake shallows, bars, and reefs. The spring hole where cold water seeps into the bottom of the lake is only a good fishing locality when sufficient vegetation exists nearby and when the prevailing water temperature is not too low for the species of fish being sought.

The best way to take the temperature of a lake is by lowering a thermometer and holding it for readings of five-foot levels. From the fly-fishing point of view casting can, of course, only be done at the surface to the five or ten-foot level. To go deeper you will need sinking lures or weighted bait.

The fall of the year is a very good time to fish and it is almost as good as springtime. With the coming of colder nights, lowered sun angles, and resultant lower averaging water temperatures, a surface cooling takes place. This acts the reverse of the spring turnover. With the surface water now again cooled to about 40 degrees, all of the lake's water is back at about the same temperature. Add fall winds to mix the water up a bit and fishing becomes great. The fish that have been sitting it out a few feet down in their cooler environment now feed and flip their tails on the surface to grab minute flies and bugs plus chasing the schools of minnows and other baitfish that are on their menu.

Then freezing temperatures come to the lake surface and the fish go down to the intermediate level. Now their surface action is over. The ice sets in and the fish go dormant. Once again it's time for the fisherman to go to the library for his reading and to the sporting goods shows for his therapy.

ARTIFICIAL IMPOUNDMENTS

Manmade lakes contain the same temperature and chemical problems as natural lakes. The only difference, basically, is that manmade lakes mature quickly and develop through the formative stages in a very few years. The same water turnover during the season takes place like clockwork. The shoreline develops its feed and harboring areas for all fish and insect life. Most impoundments are far deeper, however, than most natural lakes. This means that a lot of the impoundments' waters are barren of fish life. Way down deep, the water becomes too heavy and little light can develop the natural ecology to support baitfish, much less the bigger gamefish. So most of the deep impoundment is devoid of life and is like a desert. The most active areas, then, will be along the shore, the islands, reefs, and extensions of the bottom which reach up near or to the surface.

Manmade lakes go through development stages where the fishing is fine for a few years following the initial plantings of fish and the maturing of the right ecological set-up to foster good gamefish development. With tremendous fish growth, fine catches of big fish are recorded, but with this extreme growth the fish can become stunted unless anglers take enough gamefish to keep the numbers reduced. Stunted fish result from fish over-population and a lack of food. If this condition persists, the fishing will fall off considerably and in some cases the gamefish will virtually disappear. In exceptional cases, stronger fish will gradually take over the lake. Brown trout, for example, will kill off brook trout. Pike and musky will all but eliminate panfish and even bass. With adequate study and positive action on the part of conservation departments in cooperation with the watershed authorities, an equitable gamefish population can be maintained to take care of anglers' needs and good ecological balance.

One of the serious problems with manmade lakes is their sometimes violent changes in level. When water is drained away from the lake at the wrong time, spawning fish are killed, much silt is washed into the lake, and temperatures are varied by this water level to the point where ecological balance is impossible to maintain. Lessons are constantly being learned by management authorities with an eye to keeping such water impoundments producing good recreational fishing. An implicit objective is that the fishing be kept up to the quality of that to be found in natural lakes.

Learning to fish one of these impounded lakes one must take into consideration the changing water levels, the period of the lake's maturity, and the relative quality of the fishing—particularly the degree of balance being maintained in the various species of gamefish, natural food fish, and others.

Again, local know-how is sometimes as important as scientific know-how and, if a little luck is mixed in, so much the better.

LAKE-FISHING STRATEGIES AND TECHNIQUES

Now we'll fish a typical lake using the three types of tackle, just for the exercise.

We'll start with panfish, those small but plentiful beauties that usually can't wait to take the bait or lure you offer them. While they don't make headlines in their battles for freedom, they are a lot of fun. I know many big-game anglers who get as much pleasure from a sunfish on a 7X leader as they do from a giant tuna.

There are quite a few species of panfish but there are three main species that are most familiar: the bluegill, the crappie, and the yellow perch. We'll use bait first—fat, red worms dug from the garden or taken from the manure pile behind the barn.

Fortunately you live beside a lake, and as we walk down toward the dock we see a broken shoreline all around the lake . . . huge boulders, stretches of sandy beach, and shoreline patches where the foliage dips close to the water surface. Alders, birches, maples, and a few evergreens such as pine and hemlock show up dark against the paler greens of the leafy trees.

The day is warm and summer insects are buzzing in the bushes. The glassy water is broken occasionally by rings: rising fish.

Right near the dock where your little rowboat is tied up there is a grouping of pond lilies and grass. An old sunken tree lies out beyond, half submerged. Two turtles are sunning themselves on the branches.

There's fishing to be had even before we get in the boat. As we walk softly on the dock planks we look over into the water and spot a cluster of small sunfish.

A size-16 hook is tied onto the seven-foot tapered leader that is already on the fly line. (A bigger hook would be too large for the sunny's small mouth.) Now, hook that worm as shown in Figure 36.

You won't need any sinker here. That's for later. Now strip line from the reel and gently swing the rig over the end of the dock. Don't snap the cast or you'll flick off the worm.

Figure 36. Rig your hook through the egg sac of the worm, since this is the toughest part (or you can hook into one end – a tantalizing way but easy to lose). Tuck the tail of the worm in over the hook barb, making it more secure. Don't flip the cast. Swing the bait out easily. Very light split shot can be clamped to the leader ahead of the hook as shown elsewhere. Let bait and leader sink and then very gently retrieve. Holding your rod high bring your bait to the surface to break the film and attract fish and then let it all sink again.

Here they come – several of them – don't pull up too quickly. They like to inspect the bait, even mouthe it. . . .

That's the ticket! Your first fish!

Rule One when playing a fish you've hooked. Keep your rod *high*. Use the supple, bending rod to cushion the tension on the line. Reel in – or in this case, since we've got you using a fly rod – pull the line in with your left hand (always reaching up to the first line guide to take hold of the next length of line). *Play* the fish. Let him run a little. It's only a little sunny, and you could yank him right in any time you wanted to . . . but when you get a big trout or largemouth bass on your line it will be a different story, so start right now getting used to the feel of playing a fish to tire him. Let him have line when he insists on running with it, and take that line (and more) right back when he stops his run. Start getting used to keeping your hooked and fighting fish away from trouble – that gnarled branch lying in the water, or that weed bed over there. . . .

A whole separate book could be written on playing and landing various kinds of fish in various situations, and I'll have some more to say about this as we get on into different lake and stream scenarios. But for now just concentrate on Rule One: When your fish is hooked, keep your rod *high*!

Okay now. You play him out, retrieve the line you've been pulling in, and wind it back on the reel. For practice use the net. Submerge it and lead the fish into it and then up you come.

Gently unhook your prize and place him back in the water, don't just throw him back.

There's a bigger fish out there, a yellow perch, and if he can be attracted he'll bring his fellows with him. Cast another worm out there a bit further and let it sink. He's got it! A bit more muscle in the battle now . . . see how he bends your rod tip? Play him in and let him go.

Another yellow perch, a bigger one this time—and you almost goofed. You let him take too much line while you were fumbling with the rod. He ran you into the lilly pads. You're stuck. But don't try to pull him out. Relax your line and he'll likely swim out by himself. There, he did. Now retrieve him slowly, enjoying the feel of the action on your rod.

Next let's tackle that area around the sunken tree out beyond the dock. It's too far for a fly-rod cast and besides, if you tried to cast directly out you'd probably hook the dock poles or the bushes on your backcast. So use the spinning rod. And since the water looks to be shallow all the way out, attach a small Colorado spinner to your line and impale a medium-sized worm. (See Figure 37.) I'm not saying what might be out there . . . but we'll soon find out. Set the drag on your reel to just below the breaking point of the line and make your cast to one side of the snag. Begin the retrieve before the lure hits the water. Retrieve slowly though. It will sink just enough. . . .

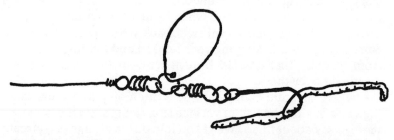

Figure 37. The famed Colorado spinner is a killer on all game fish when used properly. For lake fishing rig up a worm, live bait minnow, or pork chunk. Or fish the spinner without any bait at all. When you're using the spinning rod, a small weight might be needed for a longer cast. When working the shallows, stop the cast and begin your retrieve as the lure hits the water—and keep the rig up and away from snags.

No luck? Inspect the bait. OK try again, this time casting right at the center of the snag and a foot or two short. . . .

STRIKE!

What is it a bass?

Keep your rod tip up and retrieve slowly, maintaining a steady tension against his rushes.

Playing a fish with spinning or bait gear is of course different from fly. Instead of taking in line with your hand you're reeling in, and the way you do this is to reel in, lowering your rod as you do so, and then stop reeling and pull back on your rod. Reel in and lower, pull back. This way the rod, which is flexible and more responsive to sudden lunges by the fish, takes the strain. When you're lowering/reeling-in you're taking up slack. Then when you haul smoothly back on the rod you're bringing the fish closer.

As always, if he wants to make a sudden run away from you and bring the line to the breaking point, let him have his way and start all over again when he stops.

At times during the battle you may want to tighten the drag on the reel spool so that control of the line in relation to rod pressure is tighter. But remember to set the drag back to a lighter striking position for your next encounter, or a heavy fish might pull too hard and break the line.

Ease your fish down into the net. Don't make scooping passes. Usually there is enough of a final kick in the fish to make a fast dash to freedom. To avoid this, don't scare him with the net, but rather let him slide into it after you have it submerged.

It's a small bass. Look at him jump. Keep that line tight. You're into a real battle now. Work him in and lower your net. Well now. You've caught your first game fish, a largemouth bass.

Release him gently.

A word about handling the fish you've caught. If the fish is small enough for you to take hold of—gently—in your hand, remember that except for trout those fish have sharp and potentially painful fins which they can flare open and cut your hand with. So open your hand around the body of the fish ahead of the head and then move your hand slowly, carefully back down along the fish's body so as to sweep the sharp fins back.

And remember that with trout, especially if you're planning to release, never handle what you've caught with anything but wet hands.

Just for variety let's take off that spinner and replace it with a floating-popping plug. Let's see if there's another bass out there.

Make your cast as close to the log as possible, close enough to scare those turtles off their sunning perches.

Fine.

Let that plug sit there for a second or two. Now gently pop it, giving it a quick little jerk, and begin your retrive, pausing every so often for a pop or two and then reeling in. Bring it in now and recast. . . .

No luck. Perhaps we should wait until twilight for the popping plugs.

Got the feel of your tackle now?

OK let's get into the boat. You sit in the stern seat and I'll make like a guide and row you around. Place your tackle box in the center of the boat and in front of you. Place one rod on one side of the boat pointing backwards and the other on the other side.

As we push off from the dock we'll rehearse a couple of routines that will keep us from swamping the boat or hooking each other.

(See Figures 38, 39.)

To the right of the dock are overhanging trees. The gentle slope of the land tells us the water will be shallow.

Rig up your spinning rod with a small floating plug and your fly rod with a big bucktail. We'll troll the plug behind us as we slowly approach to cast in under the trees. Try to land your bucktail in under the shadows. Might pick up a perch or a bass.

Cast the plug behind us and as I row forward allow about fifty feet of line out. Close the bale of your reel and set the automatic anti-reverse so the handle won't spin if you get a strike. Make sure the line test is OK . . . and the drag not too tight in case a big one hits.

Now, facing the shore and sitting down start laying out your casts to the shoreline. Shoot in between the tree branches if you can, and allow the fly to rest and sink a bit. The forward movement of the boat will offer just enough motion to activate the fly.

If you overshoot, you'll hook your first tree. But even the experts do that once in a while, so don't worry. Learn to control

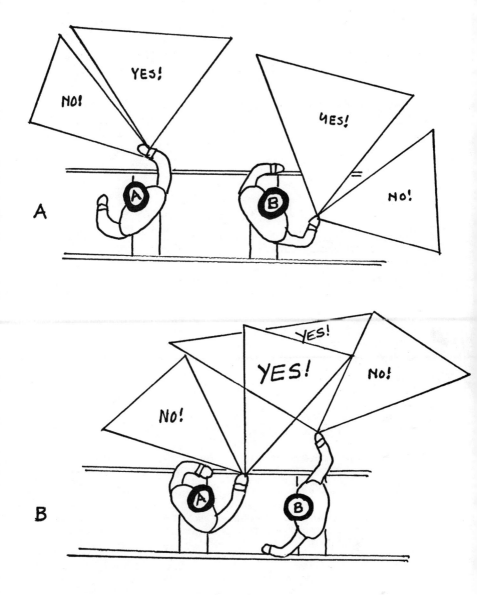

Figure 38.

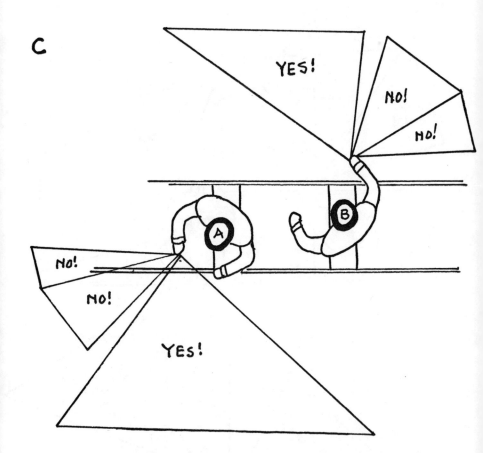

Figure 38. Let's not kill each other. Angler A should never allow his back-cast to come anywhere near angler B and vice versa. Study the NO areas carefully and remember them when you are aboard and ready to fish. Actually the two YES areas overlap and this calls for alternating casts when you are working straight out from the boat and both fishing the same side. B shows both of you facing each other and in danger of catching each other in the neck or at least tangling rods and lures in the air. So remember: alternate casts. Study the NOs. C shows the most dangerous combination—when you are working both sides of the boat. It is easy to forget the other fellow so watch this one carefully. There is plenty of safe angle to cast even if you are casting at the same time.

NOTE: While it is possible for two to stand in a boat, this is not the best idea. Best one stand while the other sits—and then alternate.

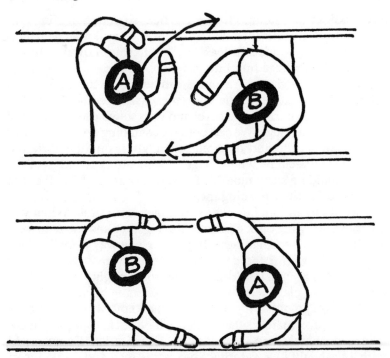

Figure 39. When you wish to change positions in a small boat, great care must be taken so as not to tangle rods, tip the boat, or hate each other. The movement should be simultaneous. Angler A begins to rise off his seat and heads for the side indicated by the arrow. Angler B heads for the other side. You may bump as you pass but in one smooth motion the boat has at all times been in complete balance and the changeover is easy. Naturally, rods and tackle boxes are set well aside from the action with the rods behind each angler and pointed away from the action. Try this a few times while in port and it will be easy even in a stiff wind and pesky waves.

your cast by overcasting and snubbing the line before the fly goes too far. This will plop it down directly where you want it. Be ready for a strike and have extra line in your hand to cushion the blow and remember to keep that rod *up*.

OOPS! Something's grabbed the plug. I'll handle the rod while you bring in your rig. Get set now and here's your battle. Nice fish of some kind. There's the jump. A bass. Play him in gradually. Look at him jump! I'll turn the boat so you're fighting him broadside. Careful when he gets close. They'll fool you into thinking they're done and then burst out again. Lower your net now and gently urge him into it. . . .

Later, at twilight, we're out again working the edges of a middle-of-the lake grass shallow generously decorated with lily pads. Possibles here are pickerel and bass so we use our fly rods and the popping bugs. We can both cast standing if we're careful.

The lake is calm and quiet and the night is ours to work that shoreline, especially where it gets deep off those rock cliffs. There should be some monster bass either already lying there or coming in for their evening meal.

A word of caution. Summer is thunderstorm time. When you see those growling dark clouds begin to gather and move toward you it's time to return to base. If you're a long way from the dock leave early, even if the dead calm seems to invite you to stay longer. Even a small lake can whip up some mighty waves. Also, the lake is no place to be when the lightening begins.

When you go out at night let someone know where you're going and approximately what time you'll be back, especially if the lake is large and there are few signs of civilization. Go equipped with a flashlight in a watertight bag, some food and drink, insect repellant, a small firstaid kit, a pair of small pliers, a hook disgorger, adequate anchor line, a hat, and a knife. This may seem like a lot of paraphernalia—until you lose a fish because you were ill-equipped!

If you're fishing in a midday windblown situation, limit your tackle to spinning and/or bait-casting. You can cast with the spinning rig and troll with the bait-casting rod or use two spinning outfits if you like. Flies are best used with calm weather and little

Figure 40. For the sharp-toothed pike and musky use a plastic-covered wire leader, a snap swivel attached to a regular swivel is also necessary to keep the rig from twisting on the cast and on the retrieve.

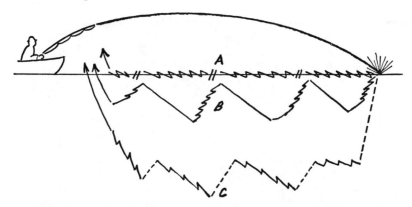

Figure 41. The actions of the three basic types of plugs is shown against the waterline. Type A is the floating plug. This can either be a running or popping plug. When it is not pulled it floats, and when pulled does not go underwater. B shows the floating-diving plug action. When left alone the plug floats and when pulled it dives. The more you pull on it the deeper it goes, usually a zigzag fashion. C shows the path of a sinking plug: sinks when left alone and when pulled zigzags upward.

or no wind. Also, bass are more prone to hit flies when it is dark or nearly so. So troll deep or still-fish with bait until the wind subsides.

In selecting your plugs remember the three basic lure actions as shown in Figure 41, and select the one that is appropriate to the situation at hand.

If you are lucky enough to have an outboard motor, use it wisely. Do not drive up full-power to the area you wish to fish. The motor vibration and wave action caused by your speed will scare any fish down for good. Approach the area by dropping your speed to almost nothing and idle in fairly close to the fishing area. Row or paddle in for your casting. If you troll with the

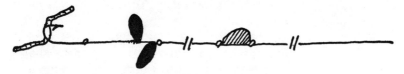

Figure 42. A simple trolling rig, similar to those shown in the chapter on terminal tackle, with trolling fin and Indiana Spinner.

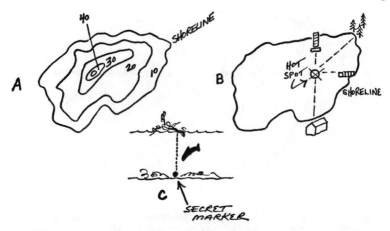

Figure 43. A shows a typical lake bottom in elevations. The contour lines denote the depth of the water and you can find your hot spots, especially the deep areas that are likely to contain springs and underwater cool currents, by studying the similar contour lines on a geodetic map. B shows how to mark a hot spot so as to be able to locate it another time. Line up the stern of your boat with a landmark, square off, and if possible include an opposite mark to go by. When you locate a really good spot, you can also place a tree branch tied to a sinker as a marker that will not be noticed by your competition for what it is (C).

motor, keep both speed and wake to a minimum. When trolling with a motor it's best to troll your lures quite a way back behind you, say at least 150 feet.

You'll learn many things by trial and error. You'll learn the hot spots and lean spots of a lake during given times of the year. You can find out the depth and shallows of a given lake by obtaining a geodetic map of the area. You can locate the underwater springs for summer deepwater still-fishing and mark where they are as shown in Figure 43.

The direction of the wind is important. Try and pick a day and a time of day when the wind is blowing across the areas you intend to fish instead of blowing right into them. All fish tend to stay down and inactive when the waves are biting at the shoreline. If the wind forces you to, stillfish instead of trolling and casting (unless your trolling is deep down). Also, drift-still-fishing is a very good way to cover the water when it's windy. Use lightly-weighted bait and allow it to sink well down and drift with the wind. If the wind is blowing right into your fishing area, find a stretch of lake that is out of the wind and return to the favored spot when conditions are better.

Early morning and twilight are the best times to fish, since a certain amount of shadow will be on the water and cooling conditions favor fish action.

Now. On the following pages we're going to try out some different lake-fishing situations—in all cases remembering to stop the boat and let the wake subside before trolling or paddling in to the spot we intend to fish.

Let's go!

SHARP POINT OF LAND

Troll: --------
Cast: ►
Still-fish: ◉

PADS
WEEDS

DEEP ROCKY SHORE

DEEP

SHALLOWS
ROCKS

WEED-MUCK SHORE

MEDIUM SHALLOW

STOP HERE
TROLL IN

SHARP POINT OF LAND

Stop your boat and pause a few moments before going ahead as indicated. Armed with your spinning rod and fly rod, proceed to the end of the point of land. Make your casts directly to the shoreline using surface plugs. You can rig for trolling along the entire route, using floating plugs that will not snag when you pause to cast. Work that deep rocky shore well, landing your lures right at the shoreline, particularly if there are snags and downed trees and overhangs from big trees. As you proceed to the pads and weeds you can throw small floating lures and even try some casts with bucktails and bass bugs or dry-fly hair flies. The shallows are holding places for big bass and pickerel with a chance at some nice crappies and bluegills. Pause and stillfish here at the edge of the deep using live minnows.

Your return up the course can include more casts from farther away from the shore. If you prefer, merely troll, a lure on the surface and another rigged for deeper running. As you round the point of land cast a few bucktails in around those rocks and stop and still-fish as indicated.

The course around the left side of the point is similar.

As the evening progresses work that point! Work it back and forth slowly casting everything in the book!

DEEP SHADY INLET COVE

Trolls: — — —
Casts: ▶ ◉
Still-fish: ⋯⋯⋯

MUSHY PADS-GRASS

SHALLOW GRASS

SINK BANK

DRIFT

STOP HERE
MOVE IN SLOWLY

DEEP SHADY INLET COVE

This layout is the reverse of the point of land but can be handled in somewhat the same manner. Stop, pause, and proceed as usual. This is an area that is just built for casting. And it's narrow enough to accommodate casting from both sides of the boat —though it would be better for both fishermen to cast to the same bank using different lures. Or one angler can cast spinners while the other flycasts into the edges of those grassy shallows, throwing either bucktails (if the wind is ruffling the water) or bass bugs (if it's quiet).

Try to work this area when the wind is not rushing waves into it. Try to work it in the morning or evening shadows and cool.

Anchor offshore from the mushy pads and grass. A small spring or brook is bringing in colder water. This is a haven for crawfish, insect life, minnows, and young game fish. You must proceed into this hot spot very slowly. Any big bass that hear or see you coming will swim right out beside you and you will be fishing over barren waters.

On the right side you have an entirely different shoreline and a deep bank bottom. Here you can drop your sinking plugs and spoons right to the water's edge and retrieve them deep. This is also a good spot for still fishing.

The center spot for still fishing is shown because this is the main highway for the big fish to enter the inlet. They should pass right underneath your boat!

Also you might want to do some drift-still-fishing as shown. Sink your bait deep and just relax and drift. . . .

But the area where that stream/spring is feeding into the shallows is your real hot spot. Go slowly, concentrate, plan ahead what your strategy will be, and fish it well.

ROCKY SHORE LINE

Troll:
Cast:
Still-fish:
Surface rocks:
Underwater rocks:

STOP
TROLL IN

DEEPER WATER

ROCKY SHORE LINE

This kind of shoreline is not easy to fish, particularly if you are in a hurry. Pick a time when it is in shadow and the wind is not rushing in on it. It is a good area in the middle of the day, but much better at night or twilight. You can troll as well as cast. Spoons are very good here, even though they sink fast. A lure with a revolving blade also is good. If the water is calm and windfree, stand up and flycast your bucktails in between the rocks letting them sink a bit before retrieving in jerks.

Nightfall will require your switching to bugs and/or floating plugs. Test your targeting and casting accuracy. Try bouncing the plugs and lures off those rocks and if there are some tantalizing snags along shore move into a comfortable casting distance and give 'em a whirl. Don't be afraid to risk getting hung up!

Bass and pike like this kind of shoreline and will generally move into it in the early evening. It is a wondrous kind of water for night casting.

To wait out the setting sun, try stillfishing at the three spots indicated, or better, drift-still-fish if the wind will take you along slowly.

MID-LAKE WEED BED

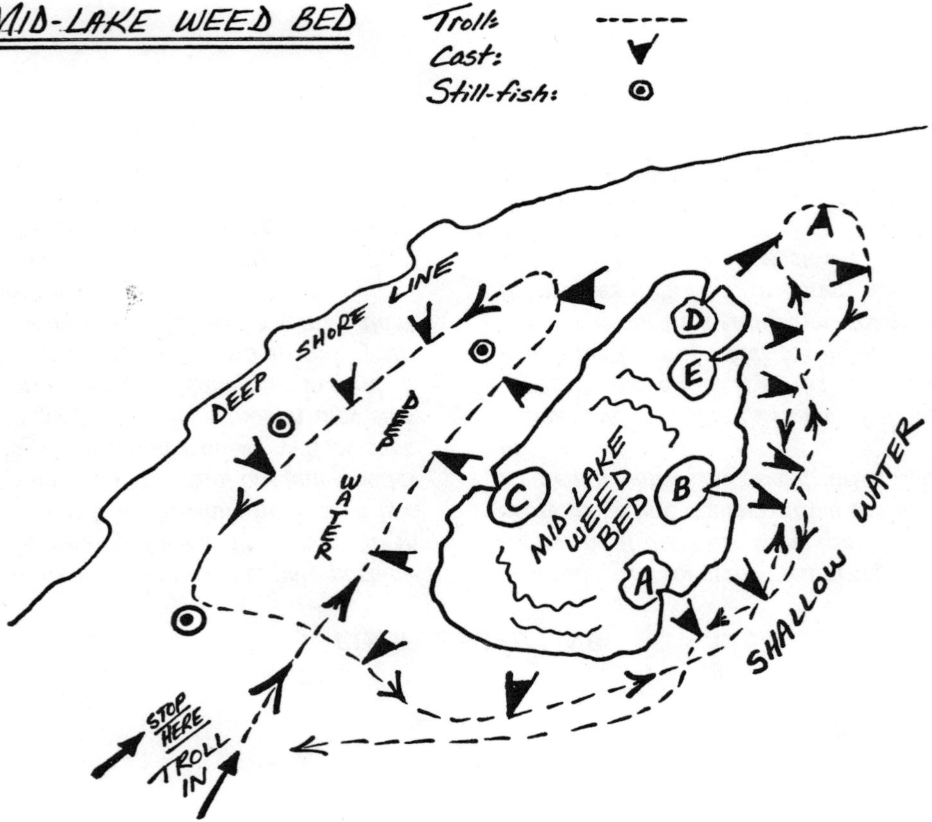

Troll:
Cast:
Still-fish:

SHALLOW WATER

MID-LAKE WEED BED

A
B
C
D
E

DEEP SHORE LINE

WEED BED

STOP HERE
TROLL IN

MID-LAKE WEED BED

If your lake contains a shallow mid-lake weed bed you are fortunate. There will be a concentration of big fish therein, particularly bass. Also, the fish that are roaming the lake will find this area in their travels and stop in for a snack. Night fishing is best here. But even during the day, if you are quiet enough in your approach, you should be able to make one of those hidden bass strike out at your lure.

If the water is ruffled, troll all the way around and cast at a few inviting breaks in the weeds. Troll deep at first without pausing to cast and this will give you a look at the hot spots to cast to later. On one side the water is deep and trolling and still-fishing are the order of the day when the wind is up. The shallow side can be worked when the water surface has calmed down a bit.

The little openings and holes in the mid-lake weeds (A, B, C, D, E) are particularly hot spots for the accurate caster. You know you are risking getting snagged and you probably will a few times, but if you can land a floating plug or even a fly-rod bug right in the center of one of those holes, you'll likely connect with a whopper.

In any shoreside situation, accurate casting and an ability to judge distances are essential. To be effective the lure must be placed as near the objective as possible. Cast in as close to shore as you can. Bass and pickerel hide in there close to the bank and a cast that is delivered well out from them won't even be noticed. Hit 'em on the head! And when you cover an area, don't make all your casts from the same position. A lure or streamer cast to exactly the same point where nothing happened the first time—but this time cast from, and retrieved at, a different angle—will often achieve success.

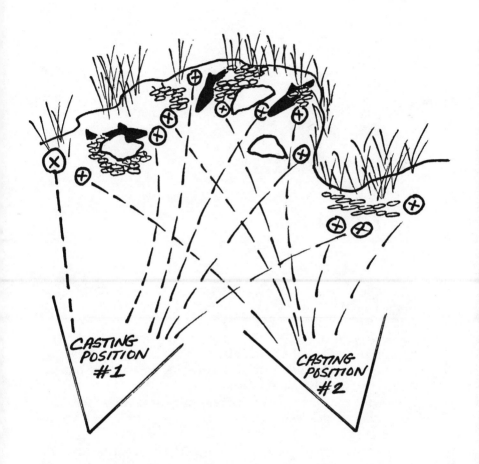

9

River Fishing

WHILE IT IS sometimes possible to get to the hot spots of a river by casting from shore, you're better off going out in a boat. Spinning tackle is the preferred rig, though at times you might want to troll with a bait-casting rod.

A few basic fundamentals apply to river fishing. First of all remember that fish, like humans, don't like to work needlessly. They seek out the river bends, backwaters, bayous, and quieter waters below or beside the faster stretches.

Look for the underwater shelves—dropoffs—where bait fish like to congregate. These bait-fish schools will draw the big boys in you can bet.

Work your lures deep, risking snags. Fly-rod poppers and surface plugs are useful at dawn or twilight, and of course after nightfall.

Bridges, docks, and piers are also potential hot spots.

You will want to tailor your delivery and retrieve to different situations. But in general remember that the across-current retrieve is best. A fish can see a lure passing by him sideways better than he can spot one going up- or down-river.

The slower river areas, where drift and muck develop into shallows and weed beds, are breeding grounds for insects and bait fish and also hiding places for the bigger fish.

The rocky areas ahead of a turn in the river are also hot spots if the current isn't too strong. Fish will hold in those rocky areas, or at least visit them during early morning and twilight feeding.

When the water is summer-hot the more active water behind drop-offs and along gravel beaches are good spots to fish, especially at night.

If you're wading, be very careful. Silt and mud often collect to make a quicksand-like bottom . . . and there are sudden holes. It's essential to use a wading staff, and when in doubt, poke your way along like a blind person.

When fishing from a boat try working your way upstream a little at first. This will give you an idea of where the currents and slack waters are, even if no surface signs make them obvious. The slack waters are what you want to fish. The faster water is your traveling lane, which you use to keep from scaring the fish out of the slower spots.

When fishing downstream from a boat (which is what you'll be doing most of the time), use a light anchor as a drag to keep you from moving too fast. Drag it from the bow—if you want to get tricky you can even use it to steer!

Now let's look at one or two river situations to give you a feel for this kind of angling.

Unless the river has dramatically changed, this is a stretch of water along the Upper Susquehanna in Pennsylvania that I have fished many times for smallmouth bass. The river is about a hundred yards wide here and the main current sweeps broadly down the righthand side of the illustration.

While it is possible to wade this stretch in July and August, better to work it with a small row boat or canoe.

Arrive at this water about an hour before sundown with your spinning gear and a stout fly rod to cast those fluffy bass bugs. If you arrive early you can anchor and still-fish the hot spots with bait.

The main exercise here is to look over the water and pinpoint the hot spots and decide how you will fish them and with what kind of gear.

Start at 1 and work your way upstream slowly to get the lay of the water. Work the shallows below that first rock cluster. Turn to 2 and cast to that grassy and rocky shoreline. Moving from 2 to 3 you move into a rock cliff area. Here there are big sunken boulders and a lot of deep water for lure casting. You can cast into the backwater slack on your left and work into those rocks above. Proceed now to 4 where you can cast to the shore rocks and down into the center rocks that swing that current for you. At 5 you work down into the rocks with long drifts and gradually drift down to 6 where you have the choice of casting to the center rocks or the grassy shoreline and sinking lures and/or bait into the backwater slack. 7 puts you above the second area of rocks and at 8 you work the shallows below. At 9 you can begin all over again.

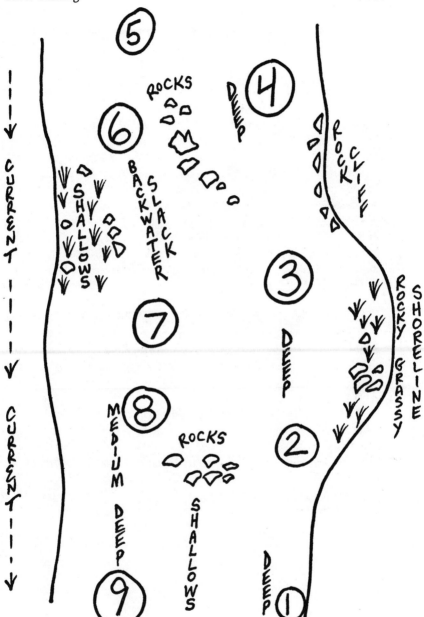

Enter this stretch from above at 1. *Note that below* 2 *and* 3 *the current sluices into a center run that is fast and heavy and deep. By slowing your boat down between* 2 *and* 3 *you can cast into those divider rock clusters. Work in close. The bass will be lying just ahead, in the slack.*

Proceed into the vortex and cast back up into the rocks, again working your lures in close. If you like, anchor just below the rocks and cast live bait upstream, allowing it to drift back to you. 4 *is another good stop for live-bait-casting and even drift-fishing as you work down to* 5. 5 *is a great position from which to cast to both sides of that gravel bar. At* 6 *you want to cast up along the outside of the bar—a great angle for floating bass bugs or a floating plug.*

Cross over now and work the left side of the river from 7, *casting live bait up into the deep heavy water and allowing it to drift way down. At* 8 *cast back to those shore rocks and snags and upstream to the grassy and rocky shoreline. As you approach the slack water try casting bait up toward the rocks and allowing it to drift back to you. At* 9 *fish down into the grassy shoreline and also work those rocks with lures or live bait, allowing the bait to circle down below you in a wide curve. Use a bobber with your bait here to keep it at the right depth.*

As darkness approaches, think about some small spinning-lure popping-plugs or fly-rod bass-bugs. You know the stretch by daylight so you can fish it now into the night. The slack water below the sluiceway and the gravel bar will be a hot spot, and so will the area between 8 *and* 9.

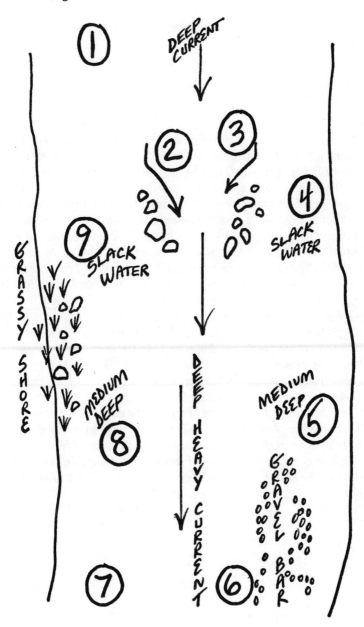

This is variety water. If you're wading you can start in at 3 and cast bugs and small floating, diving plugs all along the shoreline up ahead of you to 7. Then, if you like, reverse your direction and cast to the shoreline and swing your lures out into the current toward the rocks.

Working this stretch from a boat, start at 1 and work live bait in casts that swing into the main current until you get to 2 where you cast to the rocks and allow your bait to drift down and then draw it across to you. Same at 10 and 4, but don't miss casting directly up-current to the next batch of rocks. At 5 you can work three areas at once (with fly rod and bass bugs or big streamers or bucktails): the rocks below you, the shoreline shallows, and the rocks above. 9 and 6 are beautiful positions from which to work the next batch of rocks, and 8 puts you at the top of the stretch. From here you might decide to drift bait and gradually fall down to 9, 4, 10, and 2.

Wading this stretch in low water you might be able to work your way out from the lefthand shoreline and spotcast flies, even dry flies, by bouncing them off those rocks. Note that the right side of the illustration has been left untouched. This is deep and fast-flowing water. While some bass and perhaps walleyes might live here, the hot spots are really those rocks and shoreline on the opposite side.

This is a great stretch to experiment with and shouldn't be worked casually. The smart angler will take at least two hours to work this water.

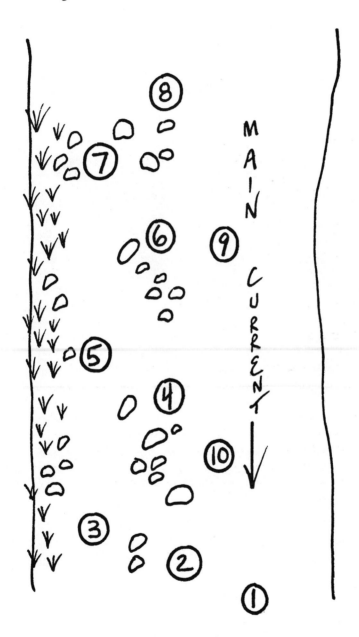

This is a portion of the Upper Sacramento River that the author has fished many times for smallmouth bass.

Fishing from a boat, start out at 1 and cast along that rock ledge, preferably with sinking spoons or spinners. (You can hit this spot later, after dark, with bass bugs.) At 2 cast down the same area to rework it. Proceed to 3 just above the island, casting and drifting lures or baits along that side of the island. Proceed now to 4, a very good spot for live bait (loaded with sinkers to put it down into the current). At 5 work the shoreline with live bait or spoons, allowing them to drift back out into the current. At 6 you work the rocks below you with drifted live bait or deep-running plugs or spoons. Proceed to 7 and work those rock clusters. Pick up your fly rod now and at 8 cast right into that beach and gravel area, preparing yourself to cast under those overhanging trees to the very edge of the shore. Night time is for 10, where you cast your bugs into the gravelly tail of the island. . . .

This area could keep you occupied for two weeks. Again, it is a matter of training yourself to look over the water first and then plan approach, technique, and choice of lures. Vary your approach. Don't neglect the fly rod bass bugs and big streamers and bucktails. Distance is not always needed. When there is sufficient current, allow your lures or flies to swing with it before reeling in for the next cast.

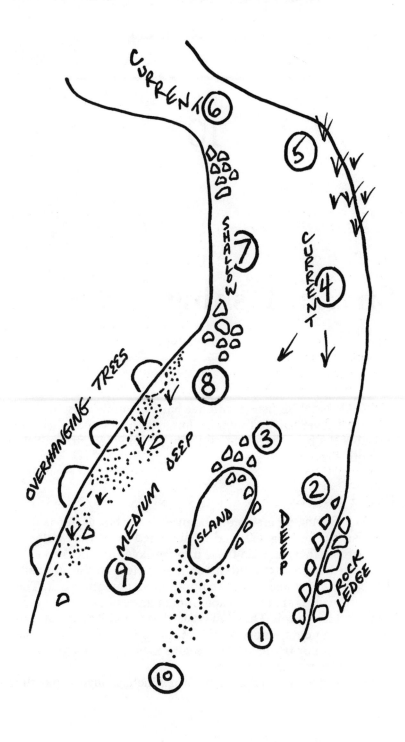

10

Stream Fishing

STREAMS CAN BE fished with live bait, spinning lures, or flies. First we'll cover bait and spinning lures, then move on to what is probably the most artistic of all fishing techniques: stream-fishing with flies.

BAIT FISHING

In bait fishing on a stream, the most important factor is current. Baits have to be cast and manipulated to drift naturally in the current lanes, and via these into the holes and pockets.

The earthworm is the oldest and most potent freshwater bait. It is easier to get and more often used than any other bait. The best earthworms are those taken from manure piles or from very damp and fertile soil. They can be used as is, but it's advisable to pack them in damp moss overnight. Keep them in a cool place such as a can or bottle and make sure they have enough air by poking holes into the container.

There is a "collar" on the earthworm which is tougher than the rest of its body. This is the section through which the hook should be inserted.

Earthworms are washed into streams by sudden freshets of water or rain. As bait, they are particularly effective immediately following a rainstorm.

Live minnows do very well too. If the belt bait-bucket is kept constantly replenished with fresh water, minnows will live longer and be livelier on the hook. Caution must be taken in handling them for the hooking process. Try not to squeeze them, even if they slither about in the hand while being hooked.

The stonefly, in its aquatic form, is one of the best major insect species for bait fishing for trout and smallmouth bass. Dobson and damsel fly larvae also are available, but not in as great supply. These last are more common on the slower streams where mud and muck roll along the shoreline. In typical gravel, boulder-strewn trout streams, the stonefly is the easiest to catch. During the months of May, June, and July you will see the empty cocoon-like cases of these insects along the shoreline of the stream. These are the shells of insects hatched the night before.

The live insect can be gathered by overturning rocks and gravel at the heads of pools and along the deeper drop-offs under water. For fishing in the early morning or evening there's nothing better than a succulent, large moth caught beneath your porch light the night before.

The grasshopper is an excellent bait as it has a fairly stiff collar for easy and more secure hooking. Best time to catch hoppers is when the dew is still on the ground in the early morning hours. They're not so lively then and they can be caught by the can-full in a few minutes in any nearby field. When fishing, throw a few into the water and watch them drift downstream on the currents. If a fish swirls the fisherman knows he's in business. Another one should be immediately offered, this one with a hook in it. The same can be done with crickets.

Cheese—bits of American and mild cheddar—simply thrills bass and trout, particularly in the Western states. And single kernels of corn are excellent bait for trout. Evidently trout mistake corn for trout eggs, or so goes the theory.

Remember, you are working with very light, soft baits. This requires a rod with limber tip-action, whether it be fly or spinning rod. Most baitcasting rods are too stiff for stream fishing.

The technique to use is the "dead drift" method. If the bait hangs in the current unnaturally it tends to spin to the surface. This is all right if the fish are very hungry, but for the bigger fish and those in heavily fished water, the closer the effect to the natural drift of loose bait carried by the current, the better the results.

This means, when casting from shore or wading, that the cast should be made in a quartering upstream direction, the path of the bait pre-planned to drift down through a run—that is by a rock, snag, into a deep hole, or under an overhanging bank. In shallow streams where the current is fast, the bait will not sink rapidly unless slightly weighted; however, too much weight and there will be snagging. In deeper, slower water, weights should be kept to a minimum because slower current will allow the bait to drop down. Only in extremely fast water should heavy weights be used.

As to the rig, some prefer the bait to drift *after* the weight, while others prefer it *before* the weight. Either way is satisfactory.

It is best for the angler to go equipped with terminal rigs prepared in advance, neatly coiled and labeled in the tackle box. This will save time on the water. Baits should be kept in containers that permit good ventilation and cool conditions. Hooks should be sharp and knots kept tied securely.

SPINNING LURES

The spin fisherman works a stream casting either down-current or across-current and retrieving as much as possible across-current. This last is not always easy to do, especially if the current is swift, since the longer the lure is in the water the more time the current has to swing both lure and line around so that your line is parallel to the current and the retrieve therefore straight up-current. Nevertheless, try to get that lure shooting across-current as much as possible during the retrieve.

The one exception might be if you're flashing a Daredevil or Colorado spinner along in close to a cut bank, in which case you will pretty much have to settle for an up-current retrieve.

Work your lures through the pools, in among the rocks, and

near any water that looks like holding water. By variation and experiment determine which types of lure work best in different stream situations, and try to develop a group of favored patterns. Generally in stream fishing for trout you'll want to get those lures fairly deep, as the trout seldom comes to the surface to take a baitfish.

As I've emphasized, the retrieve should be across-stream, across the main currents and behind as many rocks and snags as possible. The final reel-in should be slow. Quite often a fish will follow your lure all the way along during the retrieve and then pounce on it only as it reaches the limit of its drift, just at the moment when it's about to be whisked away.

In certain stream situations the spinning-lure fisherman has an advantage . . . but in general the most rewarding, most interesting, and most challenging way to fish creeks and streams is with flies.

FLY FISHING

Let's run through the four basic types of fly fishing—dry, wet, nymph, streamer—and then get out on the water for some hands-on experience.

First, the dry fly.

In order to fish the dry fly effectively a variety of fly types and styles are available. Generally, anglers like to see their flies ride high on the water and it is a necessity that the fly be dressed with stiff hackles, unsinkable bodies, and wings that cock well upright so they can be seen from a distance under tricky light conditions. For the slower water, the fly pattern can ride lower on the water so that more of the fly sits in the surface film and is thus more visible to the fish. All dry flies are touched up with fly dope to increase their bouyancy.

The dry fly imitates the dun and spinner stage of the Mayfly; the adult of the caddis, stone, and crane flies; mosquitoes and midges; and other aquatic insects. These flies hatch in a regular schedule during the year and can be imitated by specific patterns to be used when hatches are on, riding the surface as duns or returning to the water at twilight as spinners about to mate and then deposit their eggs. Conventional upwing, slanted-wing, and flat or downwing flies are usual fare as are spider flies and their variants. Two schools of thought exist; the exact imitation school and the attractor, more generalized pattern school. Take your choice.

Some tiers have decided that wings are not necessary on dry flies and have designed their patterns accordingly. Others have decided that wings are necessary and that hackle is not. Most conventional flies are tied with both, however. Hook sizes range from 22 small to 8 large for most trout fishing. Lightweight hooks with turn-down eyes are the most common, though in the smaller patterns, up-turn eyes are preferred since the strike of the hook is up rather than down.

Dry-fly fishing stems from English tradition; it is upstream casting, basically; though across-stream casting with a short drift and direct downstream casting on a slack line are used too.

Unless there is a specific rise (when the trout are breaking the surface and feeding on insects), or the duns are floating on the current, or the spinners are dipping into the water to deposit their eggs – there will be little sign of actual surface feeding. The best system in that case is to fish/hunt, that is, to cast over likely feed lanes, runs, eddies, and even into the center of glassy still water in order to provoke a strike, allowing the fly to drift naturally as long as possible.

Except in backwaters, still waters, or 'soft glides, the leader frightening the trout when the fly is whisked away unnaturally is not a big problem for the dry-fly fisherman working our generally moving waters. In fact, drag can be an advantage at times since such surface commotion does seem to attract fish to rise to the moving fly, even though the action is unnatural. Many anglers actually create surface disturbance by bouncing or dragging their flies across the ripples in short jerks.

Midge fishing using size 20 or 22 dry flies is done generally upstream with as little drag as possible. The flies require the lightest leader tippet and a delicate casting touch.

Nor is dry-fly fishing limited to the time of the rise. Many dry-fly fishermen are content to try to bring up or raise a trout rather than to search them out with wet flies or nymphs, even though the fish might be seen actively feeding below the surface on rising nymphs.

Wet Fly Fishing

Wet fly fishing is divided into three categories; the standard small wet flies of conventional design, the nymph, and the steelhead fly. All are fished below the surface, that is, they are rarely doped to float, although they are fished much of the time in the surface film.

Standard British wet flies and their variants, American patterns developed to imitate specific insects in various stages of the hatching season, have become classics. These smaller flies are fished one, two, or three to a leader, tied on tippets which extend from the basic leader.

Nymphs have been developed during the past forty years to imitate the nymphal and larval phase of the aquatic insects. These are sometimes weighted under the dressing or fished on a weighted leader. Since the active rise follows the drift of the insects toward the surface, the fish feed for a longer time beneath the surface and thus nymphs are most effective.

The standard steelhead fly is a more generalized form of wet fly that imitates either insects or small minnows or trout fry. Very few of the patterns are attempts to imitate any specific food. Some of these patterns are quite bright and their dressings somewhat complicated, approaching the simpler British Atlantic salmon flies.

Down-and-across-stream is standard wet-fly technique under all conditions of water from the largest and fastest streams to the little meadow creeks. The object is to search out trout that are either actively feeding on underwater insects drifting toward the hatch or drowned aquatic insects drifting in the surface film. Land-bred insects also make up a large part of fish diet and so fall into the category of dead-drifting insects, as they swirl in the current.

One of the most effective techniques, especially after a rain, or in the early morning and late evening, is to fish flies on the surface along the runs and eddies, dappling the flies and actually dragging them across the smooth water. The surface disturbance must imitate the struggling form of the insect either hatching or returning to the water to lay its eggs. In this instance the wet fly is fished almost in the manner of the active dry fly.

The steelhead fly, on the other hand, is fished generally down much deeper in the bigger waters. It is not generally fished in the active style of the bucktail or streamer imitating an active minnow, but drifted in a combination of swimming and drifting with the current. The steelhead, ascending the river to spawn in the manner of the Atlantic salmon, is not necessarily actively feeding on insects. He's looking for salmon eggs drifting down from above, so the big steelhead fly is considered a reminder of the type of minnow or large insect upon which he was feeding before he ventured out into the ocean.

Most of the standard British wet flies of small size are basic on American waters, as are some of the generalized nymph patterns. Only the steelhead flies are a distinct addition to the family of patterns. During the past twenty years, with the advent of over a million fly tiers in the United States, literally thousands of small wet-fly and nymph patterns have been invented. Of these, a small percentage have been given broad use and their success has become known. It will be many years however before the nymph will become standardized, if it ever does, in the manner of conventional wet flies.

Nymph fishing has become a science as imposing as that of the dry-fly-purist cateory. As a method it is considered to be much more scientific and scholarly in its exact imitation attempts than the purist school of dry fly fishing. However, there is no "class" distinction between the two schools as to which is the more sporting art form.

Fifty years ago in the United States there was no such thing as nymph fishing. It was either wet-fly or dry-fly or a general combination of both. Standard wet-fly patterns were either imported from England or tied to basic English patterns. These were largely fished in the "chuck and chance it" tradition, usually dappled on the surface, allowed to swim in the current. A few anglers weighted their leaders or tied weighted flies, especially for early season fishing when the water was high and discolored or at times when there were no hatches in evidence.

Streamer and bucktail flies were developed to imitate stream minnows, which furthered the art of wet-fly fishing, since many of these patterns were small and could be suggestive of the larger stream insects such as the stone fly and dobsonfly larvae. Today, "wet fly" can mean anything from a legitimate Mayfly nymph imitation to a tiny minnow.

Since the advent of nymph fishing, which got its start as suggested by such artists as Ray Bergman, Edward Hewitt, Larry Koller, James Leisenring, and this author, through books and magazine articles, the tying of wet flies as nymphs and strict nymph patterns have almost changed the "wet fly" system. Add to this the "flymph," as tied and promoted by Vernon Hidy—a combination nymph and wet fly to be used at insect emergence time—and it is plain there is quite a conglomerate of what can still be called a wet fly.

The school of exact imitation in nymphal patterns has all but eliminated the pretty flies of yesteryear. In their stead are the more drab and subtle insect colors in most artificials, both wet-fly and nymph. Almost every famous stream has one or more fly tiers in residence and they do a land-office business in patterns that produce on their stream and those in the immediate area. Some of these patterns are designed for specific insect hatches or minnow species.

In fact, the technical difference between dry-fly and wet-fly fishing is sometimes hard to define. Many dry-fly anglers do not dope their floating flies, but fish them "in the film" of the water surface, and others using, say, the woolly-worm pattern, a fly that can either sink or float, sometimes dope the wet fly version to float. The conventional wet fly fished on the surface, dappled or dragged across the top of the water, might also be termed dry-fly fishing.

So, in this era of much change and development by so many fly tiers and anglers bent on experimentation, the legitimate and dogmatic purisms of the past are all but disappeared from the angling scene. This reflects the spirit of Americans—that of discarding the conventional if results of better quality can be gained by unorthodox experimentation and daring.

Streamers and Bucktails

The basic principle of and reason for the streamer fly and its variant, the bucktail, is to present to the fish a form of bait fish upon which the game fish feeds. The streamer is a long fly in comparison with the conventional short-shank wet fly, though some streamers and bucktails are sometimes tied on conventional long-shank heavy wet fly hooks. The fly presents a slim silhouette in the water, the short, sparse underhackle generally slanted back toward the bend of the hook. In some ways it is similar to the traditional large wet fly used in Atlantic salmon fishing; in fact, many of the more complicated patterns rival the salmon patterns in complexity and beauty. It requires a heavier leader than used with smaller wet and dry flies.

The formalized streamer fly is tied on a heavy-diameter long shank hook with turn-down eye. Some patterns call for tails, most have wool or chenille bodies, some laced with gold or silver ribbing. The basic part of the fly is made with two hackle points turned inward toward each other to form a stiff center. Then a cheek is added topped with jungle cock. Short soft hackle is added to the throat.

The formalized bucktail is tied on a similar hook with a similar body, but the streamer part is made from animal hair such as deer and polar bear or any long hair including that from the back of a dog! Sometimes the clumps of hair are tied in series to present a wider, long spread. This fly is generally cheeked only with jungle cock, though a cheek feather can be added. The throat hackle is optional.

The fishing technique falls into basic categories. The most common and fruitful method is to cast the streamer across-stream, letting it bend down in the current, sinking a bit on the drift, and then retrieve in a jerking motion in a semi-circle until it is picked up for the recast. Good spots are casts made upstream from a central rock or snag, along an overhanging bank, or alongside a sandbar or line of rocks.

The direct downstream cast is made by stopping the line in the air before the entire length of cast is out, thereby allowing slack line to fall (stopcast). This gives the fly time to sink deeper. The fly is then retrieved in short jerks back upstream in combination with an across-stream pattern until the retrieve is concluded.

Up-and-across-stream streamer fly fishing is accomplished by casting the fly on a steep angle upstream, allowing it to drift a bit to sink, and then retrieving it in jerks when the fly is about squared to the opposite bank of the stream.

One particularly attractive method, especially in fast and white water, is to cast the fly into the most active water, then retrieve the fly on the surface creating as much of a fuss as possible by rod manipulation. The fly is literally skipped upon the water surface and raced toward the rod.

In contrast, the most productive technique in slow water or pools is to allow the fly to sink deep to the bottom, and then in short jerks the fly is retrieved slowly across the bottom.

The streamer and bucktail are always fished in an active manner rather than simply being drifted in the current.

Now let's go out on the stream and try out some different fly-fishing situations.

Let's take a close look at the possibilities here. Before you start fishing (from 1 for example), realize that you will want to work each of the rocks, not just cast randomly and disturb the water. Take it step by step. Fishing the C rock from 1 requires a cast that will fall just beyond the rock and above it, allowing the flies to sink a bit and almost bump the rock as they swing back to you. Next rollcast a fly right over the rock and let it come down into the wake. Raise your rod tip and skitter the fly as it drifts down in that wash. Repeat the same procedure from 8 to rock B. From 7 you can cast to rock A and also throw one behind you to rock C again, always allowing your fly or lure to drift in a semi-cricle across the wash.

If you start in at 2 you can cast up and across the current ahead of rock C and let your fly drift right back to you. Work the run between rock C and rock B and so on across to A.

The reverse of all this can be done starting from 6 and 5.

Practice your casting here. Remember to work your fly, or flies, with the rod tip held high so you can dapple, especially if there's a hatch on.

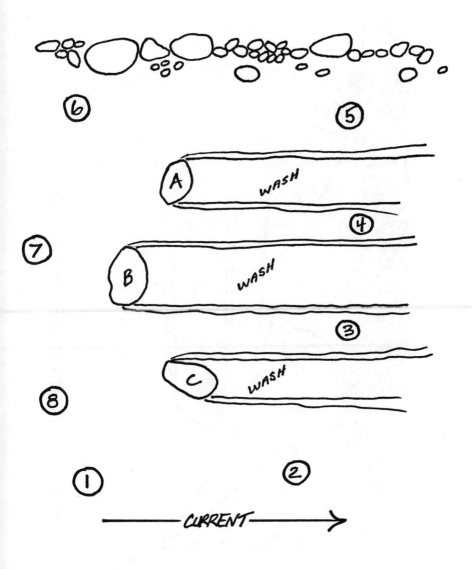

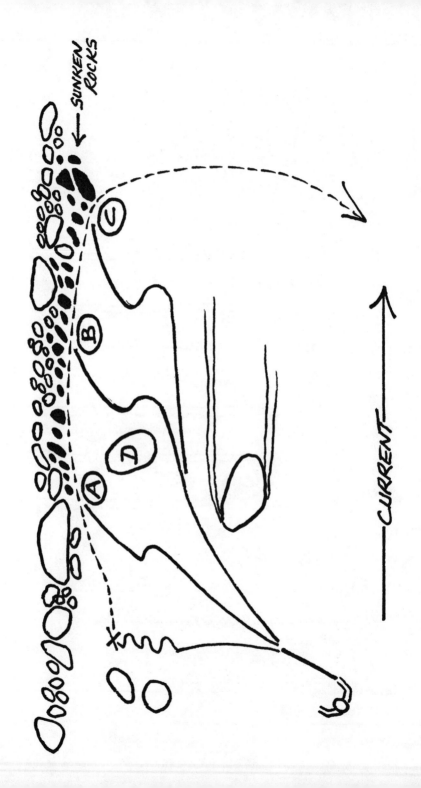

SUNKEN ROCKS

CURRENT

A tough spot to fish, since you can't get closer to it than is shown.

To get that fly right in there against the bank, cast a loose line (with plenty of slack as shown) behind that far rock, and as the fly drifts down, rollcast an extra bit of line without disturbing the drifting fly as it approaches A. Now, without recasting or disturbing the drifting fly, rollcast another length of line to extend the drift into those sunken rocks.

As the fly approaches B you will have to contend with that rock D, so rollcast another length of line right over it to allow the fly to drift down from B to C. Let the fly swing out into the ends of the rockwashes. There could very well be a trout resting down there in the deeper water.

Retrieve right back to your rod tip. A trout will often surprise you by flashing up and grabbing your fly when you have pulled in most of your line and are just about to lift your fly off the water to make another cast. So always finish out your cast and be ready for a strike.

One more thing. If you mess up the difficult presentation described above, don't worry. Try it again. Even if you've flailed the water so horribly you've put down any and all fish, try the casting steps again. Do it for practice, before moving on to the next part of the stream. Someday you'll come back to this spot —or encounter one just like it.

Potent-looking, this stream bend! Let's fish it right.

At the top of the picture the stream is quite narrow, maybe thirty feet across. At 1 or 6, depending which side of the water you're on, you begin by looking the water over and deciding on a strategy. Obviously it's better not to wade if you can avoid it.

Moving downstream you fish across and down either with light spinning spoons or a brace of wet flies or even a streamer or bucktail.

As you approach the bend your attention is on the rock Z in midstream. This is holding water for big fish. They'll hang out just upstream of a rock like this as well as in the wash. So drift flies down to Z from 6 and 7 or just above 2. Drift those flies as deep as possible, bringing them up to the surface just in front of the rock to imitate a rising or emerging insect. A bucktail fished the same way in a spot like this can be productive too.

At 2, cast across the top of the rock (Z) and allow your flies or lure to swing down with the current into the wash. Without moving from 2 you can cast across the Z wash to the rocks at Y, working above them and letting the circular drift of the Z wash accentuate your flies' movement. Work both rocks thoroughly and then drop a deep-running set of flies or lures in the current between the rocks.

Work the X rock the same way. Then work your way down to 4, where you can cast your flies up- and across-stream, letting them work down through the rocks and into the washes.

You work basically the same way coming down from 5 to 10.

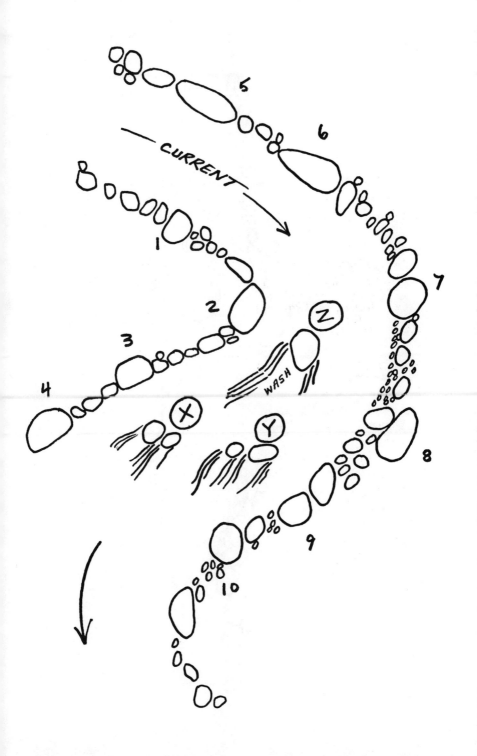

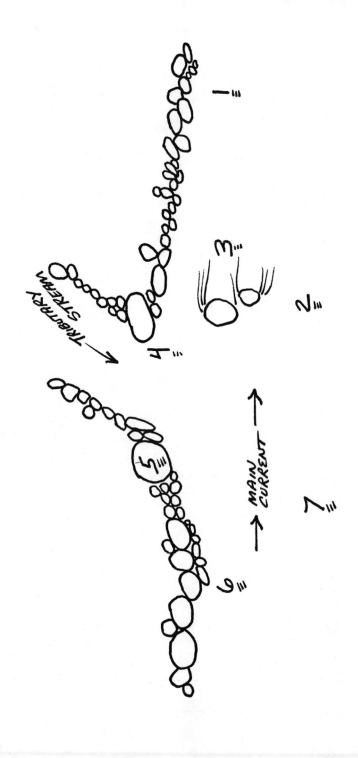

Here you have a tributary stream entering the main stream: a true hot spot if you work it properly. Say you've been fishing upstream with the flyrod and come upon this section in surprise. First things first. From 1 you cast to the rocks at 3, working the washes with either dries, wets, a bucktail—or all three.

You can wade easily up to 3 and so get a view of the tributary brook entering above you. Right on that bend at 4 is a hot spot you will want to work carefully, first with dry flies, then wets, then a bucktail (if fly fishing) or a small spoon or spinner if spinning.

After you've worked 4, wade up to it and throw a few casts up the creek and let them drift down to you. Then turn around and cast to about fifteen feet above the center rocks at 3 with a bucktail that you allow to wallow around those rocks into the wash and gradually drift back into the current between you and the rocks.

When—and only when—you have exhausted the entrance of the feeder stream, you can wade cross to 5 and open up a whole new vista. From 5 you can work the water in front of the rocks. Stopcast a dry fly. Drift down a couple of small wet flies, dapple them just as they reach the rocks, and slowly retrieve them across the feeder stream entrance and back to you. The spin fisherman can throw a long one to the outside of the two rocks at 3 and slowly retrieve through the rocks to upset any lunker that's there waiting.

At 6 you are in a position to dropcast flies and even spinning lures to make sure they sink well and drift to the rocks, swinging them on the retrieve again in front of the entering tributary.

Don't hurry this kind of water. Make changes in tackle and technique and really study the currents. You'll learn a lot for future reference. A stretch of water like this should take you all afternoon to work carefully, quietly, and well.

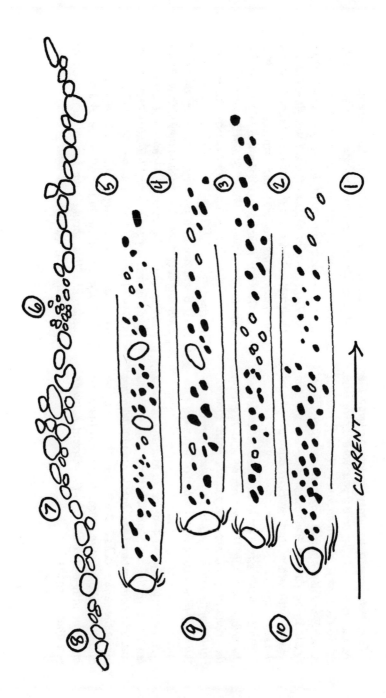

This is what a lot of anglers consider waste water: shallow, broken, and with little holding water or depth. But it can be productive. A lot of trout reside in such plain looking water, especially in the warmer season (since the water is well aerated).

Approaching the stretch from 1, make your casts directly upstream, using drys, wets, and streamers. Reserve the stretches between the rocks for your deeper running spinning lures.

No, this water doesn't look productive. But that doesn't mean you shouldn't give it a try. Casting upstream work from 1 to 2, 3, 4, and 5. Let's assume that the same kind of water is running downstream from you. So turn around and fish down to it, stop-casting your flies and lures and letting them dally in those shallow areas and looping them in and out of the deeper trenches by rod manipulation.

You might also try working this area from the shore, rollcasting with a fly rod. Start at 8 and push your flies upstream of the rocks, starting with the nearest run and moving your casts out gradually toward the middle of the stream, working the washes with across-stream casts and downstream-drift retrieves.

If you don't pick anything up, so be it. At least you gave it a shot.

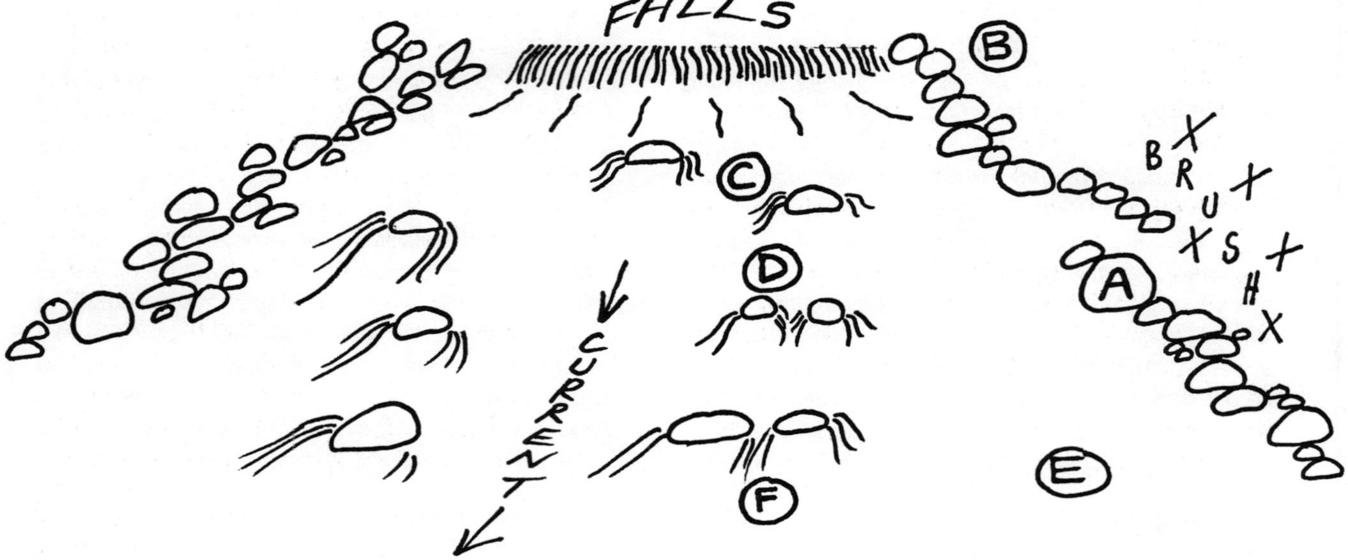
FALLS
B
C
D
A
E
F
CURRENT
BRUSH

This is a fast stretch of water, hard to wade because of its strength and force, holes that can dump you, rocks that can bruise you, and currents that will try to make your lures or flies go where they shouldn't.

But there are big fish in here. A stretch like this can keep you busy for days if you fish it right.

Approaching the stream at A, you are looking out at rocks that have speeding washes behind them. The main current is deep and fast but with generous amounts of holding places for big trout. At A you have brush behind you, and if you are fly fishing the rollcast is your best bet to reach the rocks between F and C. Make your rollcasts, with a dry fly or possibly a brace of wet flies, toward the top of the center stretch of rocks, reaching out as far as you can. Let your flies drift down along the rocks, sinking deep, and retrieve them when they've swung around to E. If you're spinning, use the same technique with a small spinner or spoon. You'll be able to reach out further with this rig, but make sure you make your retrieve fairly fast so you don't get hung up.

Now you have a choice. You can work your way from A up to B, where you can rollcast flies out into the falls break (big trout like to hang in the white water of falls late in the season), or you can drop downstream and try wading out to E. (Be careful. That's deep water and there might be holes.)

At E you can cast upstream to the rocks in the current and the rocks along the shore as well.

If you can get to F you'll be in a position to work the rock washes from below, proceeding—carefully—up to D and C. This is great bucktail water. If you're armed with spinning gear try a Colorado spinner. Don't be afraid to drop-cast your flies straight down from the tip of your rod to sink and drift down between those rocks.

Before you leave the water (going back, carefully, the way you came), dead-drift your flies through and around those three rocks on the lefthand side, retrieving only after your flies have swung out below and drifted around toward you.

Milk those casts, allowing your flies or lures to sink as deep as possible.

11

Most Popular Game Fish Species

THERE ARE APPROXIMATELY fifty species of fish above the size of the minnow in the freshwater of North America. We are concerned here with the principal game and food fishes. These two terms, *game* and *food*, often overlap, since all game species are also good food fishes. There are, however, some food fishes that are not considered "sporty" to catch. Listed, described, and illustrated in this chapter are the most popular fish, those that have won their place in anglers' hearts.

Since there are so many popular names given to fish, the Latin identifications are also included with the illustrations.

BROOK TROUT
Salvelinus fontinalis

The brook trout is a native of the Eastern states and a favorite of the fisherman. Since earliest days, the brookie, or "squaretail," has been planted in many Western waters where it has thrived even better than in its original habitat. It is judged to be the prettiest of all trout. It is a char, not a salmon. The bright red-orange fins, highlighted by a black and white front-fin set of stripes, are not found on any other species except the lake trout, which is a close cousin. The olive green back is worm-marked with dark brownish mackerel-like streaks. The trout's sides have light blue spots with rose red centers.

The best time to catch brookies is in the spring, after the ice breaks up in the lakes and the initial runoff of high waters in the streams and creeks is past. Brookies prefer minnows, worms, and aquatic insects. The sportiest methods of catching them involve the use of light fly rod or the ultralight spinning rod.

Going for brook trout in their original home, the Northeast, you might fish in one of the New England states. Here the streams are cold and clear. Worms are the best bait, though small spinning lures are often excellent. The traditional wet flies and streamers are effective most of the time.

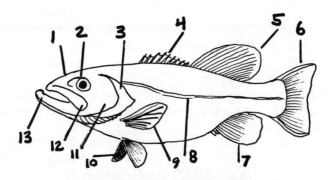

Figure 59. TYPICAL FISH (BASS)

1. Snout
2. Eye
3. Gill cover
4. Spinous portion of dorsal fin
5. Soft portion of dorsal fin
6. Caudal fin
7. Anal fin
8. Lateral line (sense organs)
9. Pectoral fin
10. Ventral fins
11. Cheek
12. Maxillary
13. Mandible or lower jaw

Brook trout grow big in northern Canada and are at their largest in Newfoundland and Labrador. During the past fifty years they have been successfully stocked in streams where the temperature seldom exceeds seventy degrees. They thrive in the Rockies and on the northern West Coast. They do not rise as avidly to the dry fly as the brown trout or rainbow. Their fight is a strong body roll rather than a long leap or fast run, such as the rainbow makes. Brook trout are treasured for their unusual colors and excellent pink meat that seems to melt in your mouth.

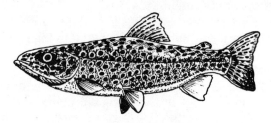

BROWN TROUT
Salmo trutta, s. fario

The brown trout was introduced from Germany in 1880 and stocked into the streams of the states of Pennsylvania and New York. The brown thrives in the deeper parts of good brook trout streams and in many cases has replaced the brook trout in streams that warm up in the summertime. They are avid risers to floating insects and will lie in large expanses of open water where the brook trout would never venture.

The brown trout grows to almost twice the size of the brook trout. Ten-pounders are not uncommon in the lakes and four-pounders are taken quite often in the big rivers.

Fishermen are thankful for the brown trout. It fights hard in a combination of surface thrashing and body-rolling. It will also leap into the air when hooked, though not nearly so much as the rainbow.

Less colorful than the brook trout, browns are equals on the dining-room table to both the brookie and rainbow. Like all trout the brown will take bait, especially worms and live minnows.

The height of the art of trout fishing is being able to take browns on dry flies.

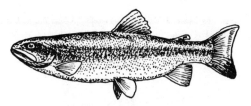

RAINBOW TROUT
Salmo gairdnerii

Before the advent of extensive transplant stocking, the rainbow trout was found only on the West Coast and in the Rocky Mountain states. The rainbow lives part of its life in the ocean and the rest of the time, during its spawning runs, in streams. In the western Mountain states it does not have access to the ocean, so it travels up and down streams, and from lakes up into the feeder streams, following its migratory inclinations.

The rainbow is noted for its spirited leaps. A running fighter rather than a body roller such as the brown and the brook trout, it often takes considerable line from light tackle in its quick dash for freedom.

The rainbow is a fast-water fish, brilliantly colored with blue silver on the lateral line with a deep orange-pink stripe. Black pepper-like spots adorn the fish from nose to tail. Its belly is pink and silver-tinged with some yellow. A big rainbow in a deep Western lake might weigh forty or fifty pounds, but average less than ten pounds. Rainbows of four and six pounds are average fare for the bigger fast-running rivers and large streams.

In going for rainbow all manner of tackle can be used, the sportiest being dry flies, wet flies, streamers and bucktails, and the ultralight spinning lures. Rainbows are easily taken on bait such as worms and minnows, especially in the spring after they have spawned and are hungry.

The rainbows' famed pink red stripe, dramatic leap, and tendency to run hard make them a favored prize for the angler. Taken on spinning gear or a fly rod they offer the most active and dramatic fight of the three trout, geared as they are for traveling up fast streams and leaping over falls to the spawning runs.

They feed avidly on aquatic insects, as do the other trout species, and are also particularly fond of bait fish.

In their native West they are the top game fish, exceeded only by their brother the steelhead trout, which actually is a sea-run rainbow.

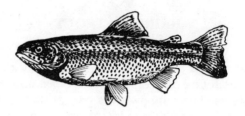

CUTTHROAT TROUT
Salmo clarkii

The cutthroat follows the salmon migration to the spawning grounds and eats the eggs that are swept away from the salmon nest. It is not considered quite as good a fighter as the rainbow, and does not attain the heavy weight or size of the rainbow, generally weighing in the neighborhood of fifteen pounds when taken in lakes and big rivers and two to six pounds when found in rivers and streams. Cutthroat are fished for mostly in the coastal streams of northern California, Oregon, Washington, and inland as far as Idaho and Wyoming.

DOLLY VARDEN TROUT
Salvelinus malma

The Dolly Varden trout looks like a large brook trout. Its basic range is the Intermountain West and north into Canada where it grows to quite a large size. It is at its best in cold, clear mountain lakes and large rivers. Twenty pounders are not uncommon.

The Dolly Varden does not take a fly with the regularity of the other trout, preferring bait and spoons and spinners of good size. Its color varies from greenish blue to a more usual bronze marked by well-spaced black dots much larger than those found on the rainbow. It is a voracious fish, striking hard and battling well. The best technique for catching it in lakes is trolling, and in rivers, trolling or slow-casting with drifting baits such as worms or minnows.

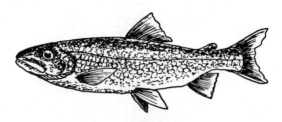

LAKE TROUT
Salvelinus namaycush

From the lakes in the wilderness of Maine to the Great Lakes of the northern Midwest, the lake trout is a popular food and game fish. You catch him by trolling and still-fishing with the baits deep down. He is an active fighter but due to the weight of the tackle used for trolling, the weight of the lures, and the depth at which the fight begins, the battle is not dramatic.

The lake trout's most distinguishing characteristic is its forked tail, which differs from the "square" tail of the brookie. Its markings are generally the same as those of the brookie, lacking however the brookie's pink and red spots—and the fins are duller in color.

Lakers feed on minnows, smelt, herring, and a generous diet of the young whitefish. They are best caught in the spring, but are readily available in the colder spring holes of the lakes as the season progresses. They have been transplanted far from their natural habitat and are found almost all over the Northern states and into Canada, as far north as Alaska. In the colder months they move into shallower water and in winter offer excellent ice fishing for those willing to brave the high winds and low temperatures.

Spinners and spoons with baited hooks have proven to be the most successful lures. Lake trout will come near enough to the surface to take flies or shallow-trolled lures only immediately after the ice melts.

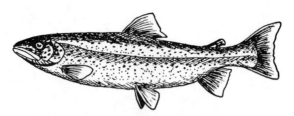

STEELHEAD TROUT
Salmo gairdnerii

The steelhead is the prize of the fast-water streams of the Pacific Coast states. You'll find all the rivers and creeks from San Francisco to Alaska filled with this fish almost all season long. There has always been considerable argument as to whether the steelhead is the same fish as the rainbow, which it resembles very closely, and it is generally concluded that this may have been the case at one time. The steelhead migrates to the ocean and spends most of the year there, ascending the freshwater streams only to spawn.

There are winter, spring, summer, and fall runs in the coastal streams, and the visiting angler can have good sport using all kinds of tackle and gear. Though some steelhead may reach fifty pounds, the general run in the average stream will weigh ten pounds or under.

In winter they can be taken with salmon-egg clusters or single salmon eggs or their imitations. In summer, conventional flies and lures will do very well. Taking the steelhead on the dry fly is one of the supreme thrills in fly fishing. They are silver-blue and mother-of-pearl with a red, rainbow-like center stripe that becomes brighter the longer they live in freshwater.

Salmon

PACIFIC SALMON

There are five species of Pacific salmon and all of them are excellent game and food fishes. They spend most of their year in the ocean, ascending the freshwater streams only to spawn.

The chinook (*Oncorhynchus tshawytscha*) is the largest and most

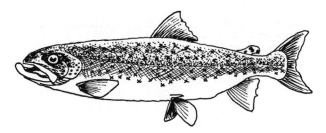

fished for by sportsmen. It is taken in the sea and at the mouths of rivers and streams generally by spoons, spinners, and the like. It seldom if ever is caught on artificial flies. Fifty pounders are often found, but the Chinook averages twenty to thirty.

The coho (*Oncorhynchus kisutch*), also called the silver salmon, is the best fly-fish in the group, according to the experts, and is taken in freshwater more regularly than the chinook. The coho is a bit smaller, averaging around ten pounds.

The sockeye (*Oncorhynchus nerka*) is only fair as a fly-rod fish and generally is taken on spoons and spinners in the ocean and inlets and in the larger streams and rivers.

The chum (*Oncorhynchus keta*) is also only fair as a fly-fish and is found in landlocked bodies of water.

Pink salmon (*Oncorhynchus gorbuscha*) is rated the least challenging to fish for but is still fun to catch and good to eat.

These salmon prefer heavier lures such as spoons and spinners and seldom feed on insects or small bait fish.

ATLANTIC SALMON
Salmo salar

The Atlantic is the only salmon species found on the East Coast of North America. It is also found, growing up to fifty pounds, in Northern Europe. Unlike the Pacific salmon, which dies on its first runs, the Atlantic salmon makes many trips to and from its spawning rivers.

It is probably the most prized sport fish in the world.

The kingly Atlantic salmon is known for its majestic leaps, which may number as many as twenty during a battle with an angler. It is built to ascend strong currents, waterfalls, and rapids, and so its strength is seemingly endless. Its meat is considered as one of the finest treats in the world. The average Atlantic salmon weighs from fifteen to twenty pounds but they can go as high as forty.

LANDLOCKED SALMON
Salmo salar sebago

Authorities seem to agree that the landlocked salmon is a subspecies of the Atlantic variety, having been landlocked since the ice ages. With its route to the sea cut off it has learned – over thousands of years – to migrate from lakes up into feeder streams.

Its range is limited to the northeastern United States and eastern Canada.

Fishing for landlocked salmon is best in the early spring when the ice begins to melt out in the lakes. For fly- and lure-fishing the best locations are at the mouths of streams. You can troll for the fish throughout the season, particularly when the water warms in the late spring and summer. The fall weather makes the water cooler and the fish are then taken near the surface by fly casting and trolling with specially designed feathered streamer flies. They seldom weigh more than six or seven pounds, and yet despite their lack of size they exhibit tremendous energy in long, fun-spirited surface battles punctuated by sensational leaps.

They taste like Atlantic salmon except that their meat is a trifle sweeter.

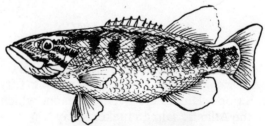

SMALLMOUTH BASS
Micropterus dolomieu

The smallmouth bass can be distinguished from the largemouth by the upper lip. It does not extend to the back border of the eye. The smallmouth is generally a slimmer fish than the largemouth, and more bronze in color, though often the two fish cannot be distinguished from one another by color if taken from the same general location.

The smallmouth bass is found in rivers and lakes in the Northern states where the largemouth cannot live because of lower water temperatures. The two are found together in most Central states areas. While the smallmouth does not grow to the size of the largemouth (averaging from two to eight pounds), it is a far more intense fighter, pound for pound putting up a more ferocious fight than any of the trout.

Both small- and largemouth bass take surface fly-rod bugs, spinning and bait-casting plugs, and spoons and spinners, both underwater and off the surface.

Smallmouth do not migrate like some of the trout but tend to hold to a specific location in a lake or stream, guarding their domain against all intruders, including anglers' lures. They can easily be provoked into striking at almost any kind of lure and tail-dancing with it across the water. Along with the largemouth they are judged to be America's favorite game fish, and on the table their meat is superb.

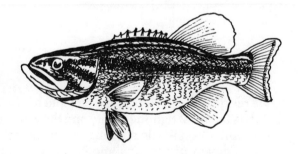

LARGEMOUTH BASS
Micropterus salmoides

The largemouth bass is found from the tip of Florida all the way to Canada. In the Southern states it grows from five to fifteen pounds, averaging three to seven pounds in the Northern states. It is distinguishable from the smallmouth because its upper jaw extends to a point well beyond the eye. Its markings and coloration are similar to those of the smallmouth except that it has a pronounced grouping of green splotches along the lateral line. In shape it is broader and fatter than the smallmouth.

The largemouth thrives in lakes and slow backwater streams, feeding on crayfish, minnows, flies, bugs, frogs, and mice. It is a voracious feeder, guarding its nest with a devilish killing instinct. It can be caught with surface plugs, bugs, flies (when the water is calm), underwater wounded-minnow plugs, spoons, and spinner-and-bait combinations either trolled, cast, or fished deep. Spinning and fly-fishing can be used, though the sport really started the development of bait-casting tackle.

Bass spawn in the late spring and at that time they are most easily provoked by surface lures cast over the spawning beds.

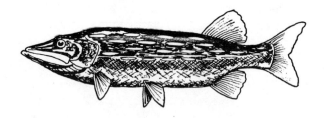

NORTHERN PIKE
Esox lucius

A worldwide resident in the Northern Hemisphere, the pike is known both for its fanatical fighting ability and the good eating it makes. In North America, pike do not range below the midstates and parallel the domain of the smallmouth bass. Deep, clear Northern lakes and big inlet or chain rivers are their favorite haunts. They feed on small fish, mice, birds, freshly hatched ducklings, and practically anything else that moves and looks like food. Heavier tackle is recommended, particularly stronger line and larger lures. Weighted surface lures cast with either bait-casting or spinning equipment are used, for the northern pike seldom takes flies or bugs, thus eliminating use of the fly rod for all practical purposes.

Their color is light greenish, blending into a bronze on their backs and peppered with darker color spots. Their weight averages from two to fifteen pounds.

They fight well out from the rod for a while and then will swim in close to you as if exhausted. Just when you think you have them licked they explode into action again.

A slack line is all they need to shake loose from your hook.

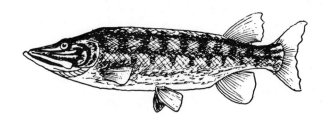

MUSKELLUNGE
Esox masquinongy

The muskellunge is the largest and most ferocious of the pike family. No fish is as fierce as the muskie. He will grab young ducklings from the surface and leap up and grab birds from overhanging tree branches. He'll take on a big carp or any lesser fish and is often thought of as the alligator of the freshwater streams.

The muskie is found in a few Midwestern states but his main bailiwick is in the central Canadian provinces. New York State and the waters of the St. Lawrence River are the best eastern areas for the muskellunge.

He demands the strongest bait-casting tackle. Many anglers use heavy freshwater spinning gear on him, but to do so successfully they must have heavy lines and heavy baits and the ability to set a hook hard and fast. The shorter, stiffer bait-casting rod is easier.

The biggest muskies are taken by casting or trolling large bait fish that have been harnessed with hooks in them. They are allowed to swim while being trolled right over the lair of the muskie. He often mouths the bait, exasperating the angler into striking too soon and thus pulling the fish from his mouth.

You don't get a second chance too often, for muskies are not only big but smart.

CHAIN PICKEREL
Esox niger

The baby brother of the pike, the chain pickerel is found in lakes and ponds all across the country from Florida into the realms of the smallmouth bass and muskie. They fight roughly on light tackle and are quite common, living in lakes and waters unsuitable sometimes even for bass. They feed on minnows, frogs, and crayfish.

Use light spinning gear, fly rods, and ultralight baitcasting rods. Smaller lures can be used too—on the surface, deep-cast, or trolled.

The pickerel's light greenish-brown sides blend into a white-yellow on the belly. Characteristic chain markings of a darker color extend almost the length of the body. Average weight is from one to five pounds.

The best place to find pickerel is in the high grass beds along the shores of, or in the middle of, lakes where shallows produce thick weed growth.

While not active strikers like the bass, pickerel can be caught by patient and slow retrieves of the lure over the spots where they live or feed. They take some time to make up their minds to strike however, often following the lure for some distance before going for it.

They are bony, but their meat is sweet and they are a fun fish to battle.

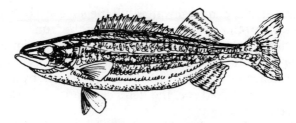

WALLEYED PIKE
Stizostedion vitreum

The walleye looks like a combination perch and pike. Known also as walleyed perch, pike perch, and in Canada as the *doré*, this table delicacy shows a great amount of fighting spirit and offers one of the most satisfying catches to be found in freshwater. While they are bony, their meat is judged to be the best of all fish except the salmon. They run in size from three to ten pounds according to their habitat.

Catching them demands a combination of still-fishing, trolling of bait, spinner-and-bait combinations, and the typical type of casting and trolling used in bass and pike fishing. They are primarily bait feeders and are not as a rule taken on lures.

Walleyes range over most of the northern bass, muskie, and pike areas of the country and are often found in company with these other fish. These walleyes are much more abundant and it seems that they can never quite be cleared out of a given lake. . . .

Baked walleye: a delicacy de luxe!

AMERICAN SHAD
Alosa sapidissima

The shad has habits similar to those of the Atlantic salmon. It migrates from the saltwater in the spring to the spawning area far upstream. Only in freshwater will the shad strike a lure, for like the salmon the shad does not feed on the "run."

On both the Atlantic and Pacific coasts, shad remain in freshwater for a month or so. They range from two to five pounds in weight, the hen or roe shad outweighing the buck by about two or three pounds. (Shad roe, the fish's eggs, are of course a well-known table delicacy.)

Sportsmen take shad on light tackle whether it be a fly-rod, ultralight spinning rig, or bait-casting outfit. Shad do not take bait of any kind but can be enticed by small spinning lures, spinners, and even small wet flies with tinsel on the hook shank.

Red and white beads strung on the hook shank will often bring hefty strikes. (Evidently shad take a lure from annoyance!)

Shad are very bony but this does not detract from their unusual taste.

Great care must be taken in hooking and playing shad, for their mouths are exceptionally soft. Play them gently but firmly and do not allow them to fight too long or the hook will wear away a hole and they will slip off.

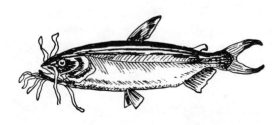

BROWN BULLHEAD
Ictalurus nebulosus

The brown bullhead is a typical catfish and one of the most common all over the nation. Like all "cats" it is strictly a bottom feeder, feeding exclusively on bait. Found in ponds, lakes, and slow-moving streams and rivers, the bullhead will seldom if ever hit a lure or fly.

CHANNEL CATFISH
Ictalurus punctatus

This is the big one, weighing as much as fifty pounds in the large rivers such as the Mississippi. A bottom feeder, the channel cat takes baits of all kinds. Still-fishing is the way to catch these monsters, and heavy gear is recommended.

Panfish

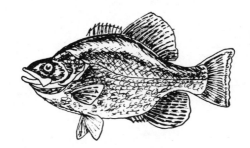

BLUEGILL

YELLOW PERCH

Panfish other than the two types illustrated above include crappies, white perch, and various other sunfish species.

The term *panfish* probably was tacked on to these fish simply because they fitted easily into the average frying pan. They were essentially a food fish in the early days. The advent of light tackle however—especially very light fly rods and ultralight spinning gear—has made panfish popular with anglers both young and old. They are easily fooled and will grab at almost anything you cast at them if you can do it without scaring them away. Found in schools in streamside pockets or grassy lakeshore sections with lots of minnows for them to feed on, they are real scrappers—though not in a class with trout or bass.

12

Keeping Your Catch

NOW, JUST WHAT happens when you do catch a fish that you want to keep for a future dinner? While it is always recommended that anglers return as many fish as possible to fight another day, it is also a good idea once in a while to savor the taste of what you've caught.

The first step is to keep the captured fish as fresh as possible. When wading, either place your catch in a creel, or a simple rope can be used to string your fish by the gills, running the rope through the mouth first. Just keep adding them and attach the rope to your belt making sure you lift it and carry it when underway. This is of course a messy way to do it, but it does keep your catch fresher than a creel will.

The metal fish stringer—a series of giant-size safety pins—is a good rig for boat fishing. The fish are pinned by the lower jaw only, allowing them to breathe naturally when placed back in the water. The rig is dangled over the side of the boat and you have to remember to haul it up when about to get underway again. The fish will remain alive until the end of your trip, at which time you can clean them.

Many sportsmen build live tanks into their boats for the keeping of both bait and catch. The "tub" is generally located in the middle of the boat and extends to both sides. It is watertight as far as the rest of the boat is concerned but has water holes in the self-contained unit for free flow of water for both bait and catch. It is covered and has a hatch door for each compartment, one for bait (such as minnows) and one for the catch.

Keeping bait alive and peppy is always part of the job of the bait fisherman and a number of ways are recommended. If the angler is wading, a bait bucket specially designed for optimal water aeration is needed. There are air pills that can be added to the water when the angler is in long transit and away from a fresh source. This pail can be left on the bank partially submerged in the water away from the current. A belt bait can will hold a few live minnows, but has to be submerged frequently to keep them alive.

CLEANING YOUR FISH

1. Remove dorsal fin and others by running a knife along the spike bases where they join the backbone and cut away.

2. Cut away the tail and ventral and anal fins.

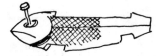

3. By holding the head firmly (nail it to wood base if necessary), scale toward the head with a sharp knife.

4. Slit along the belly. Remove head. Clean out guts and internal skin.

Glossary of Terms

ANGLE DOWNSTREAM   The angle of deviation of a downstream cast relative to "directly downstream."

ANGLE UPSTREAM   The angle of deviation of an upstream cast relative to "directly upstream."

ANTIREVERSE   A mechanism that by putting tension on the reel spool prevents the spool from spinning faster than the line is being pulled out by the cast.

AQUATIC INSECTS   Insects born in the water that hatch into the air and return to the water to lay their eggs.

ATTRACTOR   A fly constructed to imitate the looks of one of the aquatic or terrestrial insects.

BACKCAST   The back-over-the-shoulder part of the common fore-and-aft cast in fly fishing.

BACKLASH   Line rolling over itself backward due to reel spool over-spinning.

BAIT BELT BOX   A small metal box attached to the belt and used for carrying bait.

BAIT CASTING   A term used to describe fishing with multiple-winding reel and short rod.

BAITCASTING LINE   Braided or nylon, etc., level line of various pound-tests for baitcasting and spinning.

BAIT FISHING Fishing with live or dead bait such as worms, minnows, chubs, dace, or shiners.

BALANCED TACKLE Tackle which balances well in hand and also performs to its highest potential.

BARB The sharp short appendage near the point of the hook that pierces and holds the flesh of the fish.

BASS BUG A type of floating lure-fly combination designed to imitate a large floating insect or small animal bait such as a mouse or a frog.

BASS-BUG ROD A heavy fly rod used to cast big flies and small lures for bass.

BB SHOT Round lead sinkers of varied sizes, cut so that they can be clamped to the leader for the purpose of sinking flies.

BIVISIBLE FLY Floating fly made of hackles with the front of the fly tied of white hackles. The hackles of contrasting colors make the fly clearly visible to both angler and fish.

BOBBER A plastic or wood float attached to the line that keeps the bait at a regulated depth.

BOOTS Ordinary rubber boots reaching above the knees. (For shallow wading.)

BROOKIE Nickname for a brook trout.

BUCKTAIL A streamer-like wet fly made from deer-tail hairs or similar material. Imitates a small minnow or dace.

CASTING SHUCK The act of an emerging insect casting its outer shell as it transforms into a winged insect.

CLOSED-FACE REEL A spinning reel with a hood over the spool.

CREEL A willow or straw basket or canvas bag that holds the caught fish.

CURRENT Water that is moving continuously in a certain direction in the swiftest area of a stream.

CURRENT RIP A surface break in the current behind an underwater obstruction.

CURVE CAST An overhead fly cast that is made so the line hits the water with a slight curve.

CUT BAIT Sections of meat or minnows used as bait and attached on the hook.

CUT BANK A bend in the stream or lake shore that has been undercut by high water.

DAPPLING Plopping a fly, or flies, on the water surface to create water disturbance to attract fish.

DEAD-DRIFT Allowing a fly to drift naturally, i.e. without manipulating it either by rod or line action.

DIVING PLUG A plug that floats when at rest but dives when retrieved.

DOPE   Fly fisherman's slang for any liquid or greasy substance put on a dry fly to make it float.

DOUBLE HOOK   A hook with two barbs and points mounted to a single eye.

DRAG   Pressure applied to a reel to control the ease with which the reel turns. Thus, *heavy* drag means more pull must be applied to the line before the reel will begin to turn. *Light* drag means relatively little pull on the line will start the reel turning.

DRIFT   The manner in which a fly rides on, or just under, the water. Or, a manner of manipulating one's fly so as to produce a specific floating-drifting behavior.

DROP CAST   Same as "STOP CAST."

DROPPER FLY   An extra fly added to the leader by means of a leader addition.

DROP SINKER   Shaped like a drop of water, this sinker is attached to the end of the line.

DRY FLY   Any fly intended to float when fished.

DUN   The second stage of mayfly development.

EDDY   A run of current to the side of the main current caused by a rock or stream obstruction.

EGG CLUSTERS   Egg sac sections used for bait for steelhead.

EMERGING   See "HATCHING."

FALSECAST   The fore-and-aft fly-casting sequence performed without letting the line down. Used to dry the fly and/or extend the line.

FEEDER STREAM   A stream, creek, or spring entering the stream or river being fished.

FEED LANES   Those courses in the stream where the current has collected drifting insects and flotsam.

FERRULES   The male- and female-jointed rod sections which permit the rod to be disassembled for storage or transportation.

FILM   The surface of the water.

FISH BOX   A designated portion of a boat with water flowing in and out where caught fish are kept captive until ready to clean.

FISH KEEPERS   A string of metal safetypin-like snappers to which fish are attached for keeping.

FLEXING   Working a rod back and forth to test its action.

FLIES   Lures tied of feathers, thread, fur, and other materials to represent insects and bait fish.

FLOATING FLY LINE   Line for fly fishing designed to float.

FLY DOPE   A special chemical mixture applied to flies to make them float.

FLY LINE   Specially constructed line with slick finish to be cast with a fly rod.

FLY PATTERNS   Prescribed designs for particular flies.

FORE-AND-AFT CAST   The basic fly fishing cast, made directly forward (in the direction the caster is facing) and directly back, with the line extending straight back over the shoulder on the backcast.

GAME FISH   Designated fish species known for their fighting qualities and under conservation-law protection.

GAP   The distance between the hook shank and the point.

GILL   That portion of the fish's head that expands and contracts for breathing.

HACKLE   The fine feather fibers on wet and dry flies taken from a rooster neck.

HATCHING   The act of the surfacing aquatic nymph emerging as a flying insect. Also "EMERGING."

HEAD OF POOL   The water immediately below falls or downstream of a sudden slowing of the current.

HOLDING WATER   Slack or slow water, usually deep, and usually created by a rock or some other obstruction in the stream, where fish like to congregate and rest.

HOOK   Sharp J-shaped device of varying sizes used to snare and bring in the fish after it strikes the bait.

HOT SPOT   An area of the stream or lake where fish are present and active. The target for casting or trolling.

IMITATION   A fly constructed to imitate the looks of one of the aquatic insects or terrestrial insects.

JIG   A lure made of a lead head on a hook with feathers as dressing.

JUMP   Action of the fish when hooked, as it takes to the air. Also a feeding fish's aerial approach to a flying insect.

KEEL FIN   Used when trolling to keep the terminal tackle from twisting.

KEEL SINKER   A sinker attached to the line to keep the rig from twisting.

KEEPER RING   A small ring attached at the handle of a rod to hold a hook when the hook is not in use.

KNOT   The twisting of the line to make it tight and secure to hook, leader, sinker, etc.

LARVA   An underwater stage of aquatic insects such as the caddis fly.

LEADER   A strand of nylon or gut between the line and the lure or fly that minimizes visibility.

LEADER (WIRE)   A strand of wire or plastic used to keep fish with sharp teeth from cutting the line.

LEFT-HAND MEND   Type of fly cast where the line is lifted—bowed—off the water in a direction other than straight forward. Line bows to the left. (See "MEND.")

LEVEL LEADER   Leader that is one constant diameter.

LEVEL-WIND   The mechanism that winds baitcasting line onto the spool evenly.

LIMIT   The legal number and size of fish that can be taken in a day, a season, or some other period of time.

LINE   Braided line or special-material fly line kept on the reel for fishing.

LINE GUIDES   Metal or plastic-covered rings on the rod through which the line is fed out for the cast.

LINE PICKUP   The act of raising the line from the water for a recast.

LURE   A general term for any artificial contraption designed to catch fish, such as a spinner, plug, or spoon.

MAYFLY   A class of spring-emerging insect with an aquatic nymph stage and a short adult life. One of the trout's favorite foods.

MEND CAST   Used in fly fishing. An additional line manipulation by which part of the line already lying on the water is sent to the side of the original cast in a bend or loop of line to the right or left. Also used in changing the direction of a cast while the cast is in progress.

MIGRATOR   A fish that travels to a new location to spawn.

MINNOW BAITS   Any stream baitfish used as bait for catching larger fish.

MULTIPLYING REEL   A reel that has a spool that is geared to revolve usually four times to one turn of the handle. Also "multiple-winding."

NATURAL BAITS   Baits such as minnows, frogs, bugs, or worms.

NATURAL DRIFT   The way a fly or lure drifts with the current when neither impeded nor quickened by the drag of the line. A float similar to that of the real flies in the water.

NET BAG   The meshed bag attached to a hooped frame for netting fish.

NET HOOP   That portion of the net frame that holds the meshed bag.

NIGHT FISHING   Fishing for gamefish at night.

NYMPH   An artificial fly made to imitate the underwater stages of emerging aquatic insects.

NYMPH CASE   The outer shell of the mayfly and stonefly that is discarded in the hatching out on the water surface or on a rock.

OVERHEAD CAST   Fore-and-aft cast made directly overhead.

PANFISH   A small food fish that when cleaned will fit into a frying pan. (Bluegill, perch, etc.)

PLASTIC BUBBLE   Designed to act as a bobber and casting weight for fly casting with spinning gear.

PLAYING   Action by the angler with his rod and line to tire the fish and bring it to net.

PLUGS   Plastic or wooden lures of varying colors, sizes, and shapes made to resemble baitfish.

POCKET WATER   A stream section where the water slows momentarily between and among rocks or gravel sections.

POPPING PLUG   A surface plug designed to pop on the water when retrieved.

PORK CHUNK LURE   An imitation or real piece of pork used as bait.

PORK RIND LURE   An imitation or real strip of pork skin and fat used as a bait.

PRESENTATION   The technique of casting and drifting or retrieving a fly or lure.

PUPA   The prehatching stage of some aquatic insects.

PUT DOWN   To scare a fish into diving deep and hiding.

QUARTERING   45 degrees right or left of the direction indicated. Hence, "quartering upstream" means "45 degrees left or right of directly upstream."

REEL   The metallic contraption that is attached to the rod and stores the line.

RETRIEVE   To bring back the line by a cast pickup or reeling in.

RIFFLE   A stretch of broken water that is usually shallow and fast.

RIGHT-HAND MEND   A type of fly cast where the line is lifted—bowed—off the water in a direction other than straight forward. Line bows to the right. (see "MEND.")

RISE (OF FISH TO FLY OR LURE)   The fish comes up to the lure and takes, misses, or rejects it.

ROCK WAKE   A line of broken current below a stream rock.

ROCK WASH   A slack-water area below a stream rock.

ROD   A metal, glass, or wooden stick used for casting lures, flies, or bait.

ROD ACTION   The swing of the rod under pressure.

ROD GRIP   The handle of the rod, usually made of cork. Also the way the rod handle is taken into the hand for casting and retrieving.

ROD GUIDES   See "LINE GUIDES."

ROLL AND MEND CAST   Same as a mend cast but the cast is made by a rollcast rather the fore-and-aft cast, and the line is sent to the side in an S bow. (For fly casting.)

ROLLCAST   Line (fly) is picked up off the water by a forward thrust and then rolled forward without the conventional fore-and-aft routine.

RUN   A faster current stretch, usually the main current.

RUNOFF   Water from the land, usually resulting from rain or melting snow, that flows into a stream.

SALMON EGG   Pacific salmon egg used as a bait for catching steelhead trout.

SET (ROD)   A portion of the rod permanently bent from having been strained badly.

SHANK   Portion of the hook between the eye and the hook bend.

SHELF   An underwater gravel or rock formation resembling a shelf.

SHELVING RIFFLE   A line of broken water along a reeflike extention in the stream.

SHOOT LINE   To cast for extra distance, using the whip of the fly rod to pull extra line from the left (non-casting) hand.

SHUCK   The outer shell of an insect, discarded in whatever stage of transformation.

SIDEARM CAST   A cast made horizontal to the water.

SIDEWINDER CAST   Fore-and-aft cast made sideways or parallel to the water.

SINGLE-ACTION REEL   A reel used in fly fishing; one turn of the reel's handle causes one turn of the reel spool.

SINGLE HOOK   A hook with only one barb.

SINKER   Anything heavy that will sink a bait or lure to a desired depth.

SINKING PLUG   A plug that sinks when at rest.

SKITTER   Flipping flies over the surface to attract fish.

SLACK LINE   Extra line lying on the water after a fly cast.

SLIP SINKER   A sinker with a hole in it through which the leader can slip freely.

SNAG   An obstruction in the water that creates a current change or offers an opportunity for a hooked fish to tangle your line.

SNAP SWIVEL   Swivel with a safetypin-like snap for easy attachment.

SOLUNAR   Adjective relating to animals' supposed tendency to change behavior according to cycles of the sun and moon.

SPARSE FLY   A fly designed and made of less material than usually prescribed.

SPENT-WING FLY   A dry fly with its wings parallel and lying flat on the water.

SPIDER FLIES   Long-hackle small-hook dry flies.

SPINNING   Fishing with light lures and line cast from a fixed-spool reel.

SPINNER (LURE)   An artificial lure with a blade that revolves around the central shank of the lure.

SPINNER (Mayfly) The adult or final stage of development; the mature stage of the mayfly when it mates and deposits its eggs.

SPLIT RIFFLE A shallow area in midstream where the current is split.

SPOOKY Describes fish, trout especially, that are extremely wary and ready to flee.

SPOON A metal lure shaped like a spoon with hook attached.

SPOT CAST A cast made to a very specific target.

STEP POOLS A series of slack-water sections of water between falls or breaks in the stream course.

STILL FISH To fish deep, without moving the bait.

STOP CAST The forward cast is stopped before the line is stretched completely out for the drop down. Stopped this way, the cast falls short with slack line.

STREAMER Any wet fly, usually large, with hair, feathers, or other streamer-like material sweeping back from the head and generally well out behind the hook. Streamers imitate small baitfish.

STRIKE (OF ANGLER) The moment the angler, reacting to the pull of the fish or lure, pulls back sharply to set the hook.

STRIKE (OF FISH) The moment when a fish hits a lure or bait.

STRIPPING LINE Retrieving fly line from the rod, or pulling it out from the reel, by hand, or reeling in spinning or bait-casting line.

SURFACE PLUG A baitcasting or spinning lure designed to float when at rest or retrieved.

SWIVEL Small metallic joiner used to keep bait from twisting the line.

TACKLE Fishing gear including or directly related to line, lures, rod, and reel. Thus, boots for instance are not tackle.

TAIL OF POOL The area downstream of the body of a pool where the water begins to fall away into a shallow of currents.

TANDEM HOOK A second hook attached to a streamer fly.

TAPERED LEADER A leader of progressively decreasing diameter—becoming thinner toward the lure or fly end.

TAUT LINE Tight line: no slack on the water.

TERMINAL TACKLE Any tackle attached to the end of the basic line.

TERRESTRIALS Land-bred insects that fall into the stream or lake.

TIPPET The final extension of nylon or gut between the leader and the fly.

TIP TOP The line guide at the tip of the rod.

TREBLE HOOK Hook with three barbs and points mounted on a single eye.

TRIBUTARY STREAM A stream that feeds into a larger stream or lake.

TROLL To fish by trailing one's lure or bait from a moving boat.

TURN-DOWN-EYE (HOOK)   The eye of the hook is turned down in relation to the hook bend.

TURN-UP-EYE (HOOK)   The eye of the hook is turned up in relation to the hook bend.

WADERS   Belt-high or chest-high rubber or plastic waterproof boots.

WADING JACKET   A specially-designed jacket or vest with ample pockets for fishing gear and small lure containers.

WADING STAFF   A simple strong cane with a sharp metal point to use as an aid in wading difficult or fast water. Use attached to a belt by a cord.

WASTE WATER   Water thought to be void of fish.

WATER LEVEL   The water height in a lake or stream.

WEEDLESS PLUG   A plug with wire guard-shields that enable it to travel through weeds without hanging up.

WET FLY   An artificial fly tied to resemble a drowned insect or an aquatic insect's larva. Fished underwater.

WING   The usually upright feather or hair fibers set on the top of a fly to imitate insect wings.

WORMING   The use of angle worms as bait.

WRAPAROUND LEAD   A thin strip of lead wrapped around the leader to sink flies.

WULFF FLIES   Dry-fly patterns with hair wings rather than feathers.

X-DESIGNATION   Used to describe diameter of leader material in terms of pound and ounce strength.

Index